Queers in State Socialism

This short collection of essays engages with queer lives and activism in 1970s Poland, illustrating discourses about queerness and a trajectory of the struggle for rights which clearly sets itself apart, and differs from a Western-based narrative of liberation.

Contributors to this volume paint an uneven landscape of queer life in state-socialist Poland in the 1970s and early 1980s. They turn to oral history interviews and archival sources which include police files, personal letters, literature and criticism, writings by sexuality experts, and documentation of artistic practice. Unlike most of Europe, Poland did not penalize same-sex acts, although queer people were commonly treated with suspicion and vilified. But while many homosexual men and most lesbian women felt invisible and alone, some had the sense of belonging to a fledgling community. As they looked to the West, hoping for a sexual revolution that never quite arrived, they also preserved informal queer institutions dating back to the prewar years and used them to their advantage. Medical experts conversed with peers across the Iron Curtain but developed their own "socialist" methods and successfully prompted the state to recognize transgender rights, even as that state remained determined to watch and intimidate homosexual men. Literary critics, translators, and art historians began debating—and they debate still—how to read gestures defying gender and sexual norms: as an aspect of some global "gay" formation or as stemming from locally grounded queer traditions.

Emphasizing the differences of Poland's LGBT history from that of the "global" West while underscoring the existing lines of communication between queer subjects on either side of the Iron Curtain, this book will be of key interest to scholars and students in gender and sexuality studies, social history, and politics.

Tomasz Basiuk is Associate Professor at the University of Warsaw. He authored *Exposures: American Gay Men's Life Writing since Stonewall*

(2013), a monograph on the novelist William Gaddis (published in Polish in 2003); co-edited, with Dominika Ferens and Tomasz Sikora, three volumes of essays on queer studies: *Odmiany odmieńca/A Queer Mixture* (2002), *Parametry pożądania* (2006), and *Out Here* (2006); guest-edited a special journal issue on gender and sexuality (*Dialogue and Universalism* XX.5–6, 2010); and co-edited, with Krystyna Mazur and Sylwia Kuźma-Marowska, *The American Uses of History. Essays on Public Memory* (2011). He is the co-founder of the online queer studies journal *InterAlia* (since 2006), a former Fulbright visiting scholar at the CUNY Graduate Center, and a Research Fellow at Indiana University at Bloomington. Basiuk served as Principal Investigator in the HERA-funded "Cruising the 1970s. Unearthing Pre-HIV/AIDS Queer Sexual Cultures."

Jędrzej Burszta holds a PhD in cultural studies from the SWPS University in Warsaw (2019). He is Affiliated Faculty Member at the American Studies Center, University of Warsaw. His research interests include ethnography, queer theory, American speculative fiction, and popular culture. In 2015, together with Zuzanna Grębecka, he authored an ethnography of personal memories of the Soviet Army stationing in Legnica during state socialism in Poland, entitled *Mówiono "druga Moskwa." Wspomnienia legniczan o stacjonowaniu Armii Radzieckiej w latach 1945–1993* (*They Called it "Little Moscow." Memories of Soviet Army Stationing in Legnica in the Years 1945–1933*). He is also a novelist and writes for the theatre.

LGBTQ Histories

Queers in State Socialism
Cruising 1970s Poland
Edited by Tomasz Basiuk and Jędrzej Burszta

A Practical Guide to Searching LGBTQIA Historical Records
Norena Shopland

For more information about this series, please visit: www.routledge.com/LGBTQ-Histories/book-series/LGBTQH

Queers in State Socialism
Cruising 1970s Poland

**Edited by Tomasz Basiuk
and Jędrzej Burszta**

LONDON AND NEW YORK

First published 2021
by Routledge
2 Park Square, Milton Park, Abingdon, Oxon OX14 4RN

and by Routledge
605 Third Avenue, New York, NY 10017

First issued in paperback 2022

Routledge is an imprint of the Taylor & Francis Group, an informa business

© 2021 selection and editorial matter, Tomasz Basiuk and Jędrzej Burszta; individual chapters, the contributors

The right of Tomasz Basiuk and Jędrzej Burszta to be identified as the authors of the editorial material, and of the authors for their individual chapters, has been asserted in accordance with sections 77 and 78 of the Copyright, Designs and Patents Act 1988.

All rights reserved. No part of this book may be reprinted or reproduced or utilised in any form or by any electronic, mechanical, or other means, now known or hereafter invented, including photocopying and recording, or in any information storage or retrieval system, without permission in writing from the publishers.

Trademark notice: Product or corporate names may be trademarks or registered trademarks, and are used only for identification and explanation without intent to infringe.

Publisher's Note
The publisher has gone to great lengths to ensure the quality of this reprint but points out that some imperfections in the original copies may be apparent.

British Library Cataloguing-in-Publication Data
A catalogue record for this book is available from the British Library

Library of Congress Cataloging-in-Publication Data
A catalog record for this book has been requested

ISBN: 978-0-367-56336-3 (pbk)
ISBN: 978-0-367-56334-9 (hbk)
ISBN: 978-1-003-09733-4 (ebk)

DOI: 10.4324/9781003097334

Typeset in Times New Roman
by Apex CoVantage, LLC

Contents

List of contributors   ix
Acknowledgements   xii

1 Introduction: queers in the People's Republic of Poland: an uneven landscape   1
TOMASZ BASIUK AND JĘDRZEJ BURSZTA

PART I
Socialities and their literary models   9

2 Three circles of male homosexual life in state-socialist Poland   11
JĘDRZEJ BURSZTA

3 One's younger self in personal testimony and literary translation   23
TOMASZ BASIUK

4 "Transgression has become a fact": a Gothic genealogy of queerness in the People's Republic of Poland   33
BŁAŻEJ WARKOCKI

5 Queens and faggots, *Petites Folles et Pédales*: representation of Communist-era Polish queers in translations of *Lubiewo* (*Lovetown*)   45
MATEUSZ WOJCIECH KRÓL

viii *Contents*

PART II
Expert discourses 57

6 Diagnosing transsexualism, diagnosing society: the
   blurred genres of Polish sexology in the 1970s and 1980s 59
   MARIA DĘBIŃSKA

7 "Treatment is possible and effective?": Polish sexologists
   and queers in correspondence in late state socialism 74
   AGNIESZKA KOŚCIAŃSKA

8 "No authorities are interested in us, no one interferes in our
   affairs?": policing homosexual men in the People's Republic
   of Poland 88
   KAROLINA MORAWSKA

PART III
Queer intelligibility and unintelligibility 103

9 "No one talked about it": the paradoxes of lesbian
   identity in pre-1989 Poland 105
   MAGDALENA STAROSZCZYK

10 Queer (in)visibility in the art of the People's Republic
   of Poland 116
   KAROL RADZISZEWSKI AND WOJCIECH SZYMAŃSKI

   Index 129

Contributors

Tomasz Basiuk is Associate Professor at the University of Warsaw. He authored *Exposures: American Gay Men's Life Writing since Stonewall* (2013), a monograph on the novelist William Gaddis (published in Polish in 2003); co-edited, with Dominika Ferens and Tomasz Sikora, three volumes of essays on queer studies: *Odmiany odmieńca/A Queer Mixture* (2002), *Parametry pożądania* (2006), and *Out Here* (2006); guest-edited a special journal issue on gender and sexuality (*Dialogue and Universalism* XX.5–6, 2010); and co-edited, with Krystyna Mazur and Sylwia Kuźma-Marowska, *The American Uses of History. Essays on Public Memory* (2011). He is the co-founder of the online queer studies journal *InterAlia* (since 2006), a former Fulbright visiting scholar at the CUNY Graduate Center, and a Research Fellow at Indiana University at Bloomington. Basiuk served as Principal Investigator in the HERA-funded "Cruising the 1970s. Unearthing Pre-HIV/AIDS Queer Sexual Cultures."

Jędrzej Burszta holds a PhD in cultural studies from the SWPS University in Warsaw (2019). He is Affiliated Faculty Member at the American Studies Center, University of Warsaw. His research interests include ethnography, queer theory, American speculative fiction, and popular culture. In 2015, together with Zuzanna Grębecka, he authored an ethnography of personal memories of the Soviet Army stationing in Legnica during state socialism in Poland, entitled *Mówiono "druga Moskwa." Wspomnienia legniczan o stacjonowaniu Armii Radzieckiej w latach 1945–1993 (They Called it "Little Moscow." Memories of Soviet Army Stationing in Legnica in the Years 1945–1933)*. He is also a novelist and writes for the theatre.

Maria Dębińska is Assistant Professor at the Institute of Archaeology and Ethnology, Polish Academy of Sciences. Her research interests include anthropology of gender and sexuality, medical anthropology, science and technology studies, and bio-art. She received her PhD in anthropology

x Contributors

from the University of Warsaw (2015) for a thesis on the legal, medical, and social contexts of the emergence of transgender as an identity category in Poland and has published several papers on the topic. In 2013–2014, she was Visiting Researcher at the Central European University in Budapest, funded by a Visegrad Fund Scholarship.

Agnieszka Kościańska is Associate Professor in the Department of Ethnology and Cultural Anthropology, University of Warsaw. She was Visiting Fellow at Harvard University, the New School for Social Research, the University of Copenhagen, Edinburgh College of Art, and the Imre Kertész Kolleg Jena. She is the author and (co)editor of several volumes on gender and sexuality, including monographs: *Gender, Pleasure and Violence* (forthcoming from Indiana University Press, Polish version 2014) and *To See a Moose: The History of Polish Sex Education from the First Class to the Internet* (forthcoming from Berghahn Books, Polish version 2017).

Mateusz Wojciech Król is a PhD candidate at the University of Silesia in Katowice, where he is preparing a dissertation on the theoretical framing and the praxis of queer translation. His research focuses on queer and transgender themes in postmodern Polish literature. He is an educator, activist, and feminist. He spent his Fulbright year (Junior Research Award) at Yale University working with Prof. Susan Stryker.

Karolina Morawska is a PhD candidate at the Department of History, University of Warsaw. She holds master's degrees in history and in American studies. Her research interests include the history of sexuality. She has published on love and emotions in medieval Poland. In the CRUSEV study, she conducted oral history interviews on personal memories of LGBTQ persons in the 1970s and examined discourses on homosexuality and transgenderism in magazines and other documents from the era.

Karol Radziszewski is an independent artist based in Warsaw, where he received his MFA from the Academy of Fine Arts in 2004. He works with film, photography, and installations, and creates interdisciplinary projects. His archive-based methodology combines cultural, historical, religious, social, and gender references. Since 2005 he has been the publisher and editor-in-chief of *DIK Fagazine*. He is also founder of the Queer Archives Institute. His work has been presented at the National Museum, the Museum of Modern Art, and Zachęta National Gallery of Art in Warsaw; Kunsthalle Wien, Vienna; New Museum, New York; VideoBrasil, Sao Paulo; Cobra Museum, Amsterdam; Ludwig Museum, Budapest; Wrocław Contemporary Museum; and Muzeum Sztuki in Łódź. He participated in international biennales, including PERFORMA

13, New York; 7th Göteborg Biennial; 4th Prague Biennial; and 15th WRO Media Art Biennale.

Magdalena Staroszczyk is a PhD candidate at the Institute of Polish Culture, University of Warsaw. She holds an MA in cultural studies. Her interests include the counterculture and its artistic practices, feminism, gender and queer studies, performance studies, and art. Her PhD project is about the situation of and discourse on non-heteronormative women in Poland before and after 1989. She is also an artist and activist, a member of Black Rags collective (Czarne Szmaty).

Wojciech Szymański is Assistant Professor in the Department of the History of Modern Art and Culture, Institute of Art History, University of Warsaw. He is also an independent curator and art critic, member of the International Association of Art Critics (AICA), author of *Argonauci. Postminimalizm i sztuka po nowoczesności. Eva Hesse—Felix Gonzalez-Torres—Roni Horn—Derek Jarman* (*The Argonauts. Postminimalism and Art After Modernism: Eva Hesse—Felix Gonzalez-Torres—Roni Horn—Derek Jarman*, 2015), and of more than 40 academic and 100 critical texts published in exhibition catalogues, art magazines, and peer-reviewed journals and monographs. Educated in London and Cracow, he holds an MA and a PhD in art history and an MA in philosophy from the Jagiellonian University. He has curated over 30 group and solo shows and art projects in Poland and abroad, including several exhibitions of Roma contemporary artists and Roma art. His interests include gay and queer culture, postcolonial critique, contemporary Roma art, performative shift, and contemporary art in Central and Eastern Europe and in the Americas.

Błażej Warkocki is Associate Professor of Polish Literature at the Adam Mickiewicz University in Poznań, and a literary critic. He co-edited, with Zbyszek Sypniewski, *Homofobia po polsku* (*Polish Homophobia*, 2004) and with Przemysław Czapliński, Maciej Leciński, and Eliza Szybowicz, *Kalendarium życia literackiego 1976–2000* (*Calendar of Literary Life in Poland 1976–2000*, 2003). He authored three monographs on contemporary Polish literature and queer studies: *Homo niewiadomo. Polska proza wobec odmienności* (*A Queer. Polish Literature and Otherness*, 2007), *Różowy język. Literatura i polityka kultury na początku wieku* (*Pink Language. Literature and Cultural Politics at the Beginning of the Twenty-First Century*, 2013), and *Pamiętnik afektów z okresu dojrzewania. Gombrowicz—queer—Sedgwick* (*A Memoir of Affects from a Time of Immaturity. Gombrowicz—queer—Sedgwick*, 2018). His research interests include twentieth- and twenty-first-century Polish literature, comparative literature, queer theory, and the history of LGBT liberation in Eastern Europe.

Acknowledgements

The present volume stems from the study "Cruising the 1970s: Unearthing Pre-HIV/AIDS Queer Sexual Cultures" (CRUSEV), which brought together researchers and artists from the UK, Spain, Germany, and Poland as part of a consortium formed by the Edinburgh College of Art, the University of Murcia, Humboldt-University Berlin, and the University of Warsaw. We would like to thank our fellow team members: Agnieszka Kościańska, Karolina Morawska, Karol Radziszewski, Magdalena Staroszczyk, Wojciech Szymański, Błażej Warkocki, and Krzysztof Zabłocki for three years (and counting) of common effort. We also extend our thanks to the other teams, including Glyn Davis, who served as project leader, Fiona Anderson (PI), Laura Guy, Nat Raha, Benny Nemerofsky Ramsay, and Moira Thomson from the UK, Juan Antonio Suárez (PI), Alberto Berzosa, Viriginia Villaplana Ruiz, Gracia Trujillo and others from Spain, and Andreas Krass (PI), Benedikt Wolf, and Janin Afken from Germany. We thank the members of the project's advisory board: Jaap Kooijman, Mandy Merck, Hanna Musioł, and Sarah Schulman.

We thank the guest speakers who inspired us with papers presented at public seminars held at the University of Warsaw in the 2017–2018 and 2018–2019 academic years in connection to this project: Marta Abramowicz, Monika Baer, Maria Dębińska, Anna Dobrowolska, Maciej Gdula, Dorota Hall, Justyna Jaworska, Dobrochna Kałwa, Joanna Krakowska, Agnieszka Król, Renata Lis, Joanna Mizielińska, Grzegorz Niziołek, Joanna Niżyńska, Remigiusz Ryziński, Justyna Struzik, Krzysztof Tomasik, Agnieszka Wiciak, Marcin Zaremba, and Bartosz Żurawiecki. Additionally, two CRUSEV workshops held at the University of Warsaw in June and September 2018 included papers by Mariola Bieńko, Franko Dota, Mathias Foit, Aleksandra Gajowy, Ludmiła Janion, Mateusz Król, David Kurkovskiy, Kateřina Lišková, Piotr Moszczeński, Jan Szpilka, and Ladislav Zikmund-Lender. Participating in these and other events were Sylwia Kuźma-Markowska, Krystyna Mazur, Rafał Morusiewicz, Andreas Pretzel,

Acknowledgements xiii

Agnieszka Weseli, and many others. We thank Wiktor Dynarski, Wolfgang Jöhling, Adriana Kapała, Krzysztof Kliszczyński, Radosław Korzycki, Jerzy Krzyszpień, Andrzej Selerowicz, Łukasz Szulc, and others who spoke with us and who assisted us in archival searches and in other invaluable ways. We thank our fellow researchers from EUROPACH (another HERA project), especially Agata Dziuban and Todd Sekuler, for their support. All these individuals have contributed to our thinking about the queer 1970s.

We thank the University of Warsaw departments: the American Studies Center, the Institute of Polish Culture, the Institute of Ethnology and Cultural Anthropology, and the Faculty of History for hosting and otherwise facilitating our events and other endeavours. We thank our institutional partners, in particular the Centre for Contemporary Art Zamek Ujazdowski in Warsaw, Lambda Warsaw, the Campaign Against Homophobia, Trans-Fuzja, the Stonewall Group, and Pracownia Duży Pokój.

Last but not least, we thank our interview partners, most of whom wished to remain anonymous.

***

Chapters by Tomasz Basiuk, Jędrzej Burszta, Agnieszka Kościańska, Karolina Morawska, Karol Radziszewski and Wojciech Szymański, Magdalena Staroszczyk, and Błażej Warkocki present partial research results from the CRUSEV study. Chapters by Maria Dębińska and Mateusz Król were originally presented at events held in connection to the CRUSEV project.

Chapters by Morawska, Radziszewski and Szymański, and Warkocki were translated from Polish by Aleksandra Sobczak-Kövesi and were subsequently revised by the authors and by the editors for inclusion in this volume.

Cruising the 1970s: Un-earthing Pre-HIV/AIDS Queer Sexual Cultures (CRUSEV) has been financially supported by the HERA Joint Research Programme 3 Uses of the Past which is co-funded by AHRC, AKA, BMBF via DLR-PT, CAS, CNR, DASTI, ETAg, FCT, F.R.S.—FNRS, FWF, FWO, IRC, LMT, MIZS, MINECO, NCN, NOW, RANNÍS, RCN, SNF, VIAA, VR, and the European Commision through Horizon 2020.

xiv *Acknowledgements*

This project has received funding from the European Union's Horizon 2020 research and innovation programme under grant agreement No. 649307.

1 Introduction
Queers in the People's Republic of Poland: an uneven landscape

Tomasz Basiuk and Jędrzej Burszta

The history of non-normative sexuality in twentieth-century Poland is both little-explored and different from that of other European countries, especially in the non-penalization of same-sex acts (see, for example, on Hungary: Kurimay and Takács 2017; on Czechoslovakia: Lišková 2018; on East Germany: McLellan 2011, 114–118; on Russia: Healey 2001; on Western Europe: Cook 2007; Herzog 2011).[1] From the late eighteenth century until 1918, Poland was under partition by its neighbouring countries, each of them imposing its criminal jurisdiction. In 1807, a small part of the former Polish territory was briefly given autonomy under Napoleon. Partly as a legacy of this interlude, in 1932 the newly independent Poland adopted a progressive penal code which did not prohibit same-sex acts. The code used a broad definition of sexual violence, which made same-sex rape a punishable offense, and it set the same age of consent for homo- and heterosexual intercourse.

This liberal law was reinstituted post-1945. Since 1932, the code penalized homosexual prostitution but not the heterosexual kind, yet the bias was removed in 1969 (Płatek 2009). With regard to statutory regulation of homosexuality, the People's Republic of Poland was one of the most liberal countries in Europe, including in the Communist Bloc. Homosexuality was illegal in the Soviet Union, Romania, Albania, and in some parts of Yugoslavia (Kosovo, Macedonia, Serbia, Bosnia and Herzegovina). In countries which did not prohibit same-sex acts, harsher penalties were sometimes imposed for sex-related offences involving same-sex activity, as was the case in Czechoslovakia, Hungary, Bulgaria, and East Germany, and consent was set at a higher age for same-sex acts (see Szulc 2018, 72–76 for more on the complexity of the legal status of homosexuality in the region).

After 1945, queer life in Poland continued because the mostly underground informal institutions which enabled it, such as cruising grounds and unofficial gathering places, survived the war and the geopolitical transition which followed. Public baths and certain bars and cafes were frequented by the initiated at certain times, some theatre performances drew those in the know, and private parties provided the space for social interaction and networking (Ryziński 2017). Those participating in such informal queer gatherings were not necessarily aware of other such practices or groups. Grzegorz Niziołek applies Michael Warner's concept of counterpublics (2002) to the various queer communities functioning in this manner in the People's Republic of Poland; rather than in terms of sexual identity, they are defined "in terms of their relation to the public sphere, within which they expose areas of affective disruption, dissatisfaction and resistance" (2016, 288).

With some quotidian queer practices continuing from the prewar years and despite the absence of penalization, Poland's homosexuals under state socialism nonetheless suffered prejudice and discrimination in everyday life. Homosexuality was rarely spoken about in public and was often denigrated in private, including by families of origin and peers.[2] The Roman Catholic Church, which remained a formidable force also under Communism, restricted sexual mores, albeit without specifically focusing on homosexuality up until the 1980s (Hall 2016). Its approach meshed, in this respect, with that of the state authorities, which had no official policy on homosexuality but regarded it with suspicion. The prevailing perception was that homosexuality was antisocialist and antifamily, often associated, as in the USSR (Healey 2001), with prison culture (Szulc 2018, 98) and considered criminogenic (for an example of this sort of perception, see Giza 1970; Kopka 1985).

Homosexual men in particular were deemed both likely victims and likely perpetrators of criminal acts. As a group, they were kept under close surveillance by the state police (dubbed Citizens' Militia) and the secret service (Fiedotow 2012, 271–272). In the wake of a martial law imposed in 1981 to suppress the ten-million strong protest movement known as Solidarity, and with the onset of HIV/AIDS, this surveillance assumed a massive scale and became openly intimidating (Szulc 2018, 106–110; Kościańska 2017, 230–237; Majewska 2018). Police activities culminated in the infamous operation "Hiacynt" (Hyacinth) begun in November 1985, in which homosexuals already known to the police were apprehended, brought into precincts, and questioned about their sexual partners, roommates, and friends. This nationwide operation was carried out over just two days (and later repeated), indicating the extent of the state's knowledge about and determination to control those engaging in same-sex acts. Unintended by the authorities, the clampdown had the effect of spurring the fledgling gay and lesbian movement to action.

The lack of a movement prior to the 1980s was partly due to the absence of penalization, which took away a major motive for political struggle.

Moreover, the People's Republic of Poland curtailed free assembly and civic institutions. Organizations were outlawed unless licensed by the state, which had the effect of blocking official gay and lesbian activism (Szulc 2018), as was also true of other East Bloc countries (McLellan 2011; Kurimay and Takács 2017). Understandably, scholars and writers investigating the queer history of state-socialist Poland focused on the mid- to late 1980s, when the first gay magazines came on stage and early political organizing was in evidence (Fiedotow 2012; Szulc 2018; Szcześniak 2012, 2016; O'Dwyer 2018). Although some have looked at a more distant past—notably, Krzysztof Tomasik provides an exceptionally comprehensive survey of popular representations of homosexuality in the People's Republic of Poland (2012)—fragmentation of available histories remains a problem, with relatively little said about the earlier decades (see, however, Nastulczyk and Oczko 2012 for a study of homosexuality in the Middle Ages and Modern era). Our choice has been to look at the 1970s, which we see not only as an interval neatly bracketed by a change in the ruling party's leadership in 1970, resulting in partial relaxation of Communist rule at the start of the decade, and by the emergence of the short-lived Solidarity movement in 1980 at its end, but equally as "the long 1970s," that is, a decade determined by earlier developments, such as the ongoing evolution of sexology in Poland (Kościańska 2014), which had a markedly positive impact on transgender rights, and a period in which the ground was laid for a more overtly political gay and lesbian movement emerging in the mid- to late 1980s and post-1989. It was a time of intensified cultural and knowledge exchanges, as the Iron Curtain temporarily became less impermeable, of diminishing anonymity in same-sex contacts, and of a gradual lifting of the silence veiling homosexuality. For these reasons, Magda Szcześniak has referred to a "proto-gay" era (Szcześniak 2016) and one of the editors has described the 1970s and early 1980 as "proto-political" (Basiuk 2019).

These positive developments were limited to urban centres, however, and were marginal even there. A number of interview partners contributing to our project have reported that they had little sense of a bigger queer community in the 1970s and 1980s, and that finding another queer person was sometimes a challenge. This was especially the case for women, who did not have informal queer spaces at their disposal, the way men did as a group, and who were often unaware of the very existence of other lesbians. Women seem to have met partners and lovers in coincidental encounters taking place in otherwise heteronormative contexts, such as the workplace. As one interview partner put it: "in the 1970s I was so lonely, I didn't know any other lesbian, except for one, who also only knew me."

No doubt one reason for this painful invisibility was that the Western sexual revolution of the late 1960s and the 1970s had limited resonance

4 *Tomasz Basiuk and Jędrzej Burszta*

in Poland. Despite efforts by experts, journalists, literary translators, and others who depicted the shifting sexual mores, and despite some representations being made available in the popular media, Poland did not undergo a comparable social and cultural change. A very marginal hippie movement was all but inconsequential, while the Polish 1968 student revolt had an entirely different trajectory than in France or West Germany (Garsztecki 2008, 184). It is altogether unsurprising that Poland is mentioned only in the narrow context of access to abortion and of condom use by contributors to Gert Hekma's and Alain Giami's *Sexual Revolutions* (2014) and only in the former context in Dagmar Herzog's study of sexuality in twentieth-century Europe (2011).

Like any history of sexuality, this collection faces the challenge of shifting terminologies. Contributors use a range of terms to render social and epistemological contexts and to build bridges between the past and the present, as well as between the Polish and the English language. Expressions common nowadays, such as *osoba homoseksualna* (a homosexual person), *osoba nieheteronormatywna* (a non-heteronormative person), *transpłciowość* (transgender), and *homoseksualność*, rather than *homoseksualizm* (both words refer to homosexuality but the latter is openly medicalizing, similar to the difference between "homosexualism" and "homosexuality"), are recent coinages. In the 1970s, the word *homoseksualista* (a homosexual) was used but many chose euphemisms or camp terms, such as feminine endings applied to male persons, to refer to themselves and others (Burszta 2019; Nowak 2019). A common, offensive term for a homosexual man was *pedał* (a near-homonym of the French *pédé* but literally meaning "pedal"), while the nominally neutral *lesbijka* (lesbian) doubled as a slur. The terms *transseksualista* (transsexual) and *transwestyta* (transvestite) functioned as near-synonyms. The word *gej* (gay) was introduced in the 1980s and became common in the 1990s, popularized by gay and lesbian activists (see Szulc 2012, 73–79).

Contributors to this volume occasionally use "gay" with reference to the 1970s in a consciously anachronistic way, analogous to such word choice made, for example, by historian John Boswell (1980). (Of course, in the 1970s, the word *gay* did function in English with the meaning used here; for more on the entangled chronologies of queer discourses in Central and Eastern Europe see Kulpa and Mizielińska 2016.) The word "queer"—sometimes translated into the Polish as *odmieniec*, meaning one who is different or transformed (Basiuk 2000)—is used here polysemically. It is an umbrella term for a wide range of gender and sexual nonconformity, a partly archaic and/or offensive term for a male homosexual (e.g. Paweł Lipszyc translated William Burrough's *Queer* as *Pedał*), and, crucially, the term used by Douglas Crimp in his "queer before gay" project (the original title of Crimp's study of Andy Warhol's films, published as *Our Kind of Movies*,

2012; see also Danbolt 2008). This last usage, "queer before gay," most closely approximates our project and corresponds to the meaning of "queer" in the title of the present volume. This sense of "queer" is also implied in the subtitle of the international study from which our volume stems, "Cruising the 1970s: Unearthing Pre-HIV/AIDS Queer Sexual Cultures." The word *pikieta* (cruising grounds), which continues to be used and which derives from the picket line, thus implying dissent, participates in something like the "queer before gay" paradigm suggested by Crimp.

Those of us "cruising" the 1970s in Poland faced the particular challenge posed by the relative dearth of archival material and its physical dissipation, as well as the absence of a comprehensive history of homosexuality and transgenderism in Poland, including in the postwar years. The first kind of challenge required us to scout for archival material and conduct more than 40 oral history interviews. Contributors to this volume rely on various archives, including court documents, state police papers, expert discourses on sexuality, literary criticism, epistolography, visual arts, and oral history interviews. The second challenge meant we had to begin *in medias res*, without an authoritative historical account on which to build our argument. While a number of excellent studies have been produced to date, many of them already mentioned, the historical landscape they jointly paint remains fragmented. Researching the queer past of state-socialist Poland has therefore had the distinct flavour of "cruising" in the sense given this term by José Esteban Muñoz (2009): we were finding—and are offering here—glimpses of a queer utopia, or perhaps, queer heterotopia (Foucault 1986). Unexpected and often surprising, they inevitably complicate and partly bely the era's largely dystopian image.

Part I, "Socialities and their literary models," consists of four chapters. Drawing on oral history interviews, Jędrzej Burszta reconstructs three circles of male homosexual social life in socialist Poland: the cruising spaces used for anonymous same-sex sex acts (public restrooms, parks etc.), the public bathhouses, ascribed with homosocial and homoerotic meanings and practices, and the specific counter-institution of "gay parlours," that is, the space of private apartments used for socializing, networking, and transferring knowledge. Burszta discusses how each type of queer space is affectively remembered as a site of non-normative expressions of identity, desire, and emerging (proto-)political organization. Tomasz Basiuk proposes a queer reading of two testimonials—a letter from one Polish gay-male activist to another and an oral history interview with a retired homosexual man—which share the strategy of referencing translated work by queer writers. Basiuk contends that these testimonials illustrate Eve Kosofsky Sedgwick's argument that queer transformational energy is mobilized by an interest in one's younger self. Błażej Warkocki traces the Gothic genealogy of queerness in Polish literature to the anthologies published in the book series *Transgresje* (*Transgressions*), a queer archive and a variant of queer theory by the influential literary scholar Maria Janion. Mateusz Król compares the French and English translations of the postmodern queer novel *Lubiewo* (*Lovetown*) by Michał Witkowski. Considered a transgressive game-changer in Polish literary culture, the book juxtaposes the lives of pre-emancipatory, anti-assimilationist queers from "the long 1970s" with those of pro-emancipatory, Westward-oriented gay men from the 1990s.

Part II, "Expert discourses," examines the concepts of gender and sexuality used by sexologists, lawyers, and the police. Maria Dębińska discusses the official approach to gender nonconformity in pre-1989 Poland as informed by the ideology of socialist humanism and providing individuals diagnosed as transsexual with state-funded medical care and a relatively simple legal procedure for changing their documents. Dębińska suggests that the opposition between medicalization and emancipation was irrelevant under socialist humanism. Agnieszka Kościańska focuses on the correspondence between the sexologist Zbigniew Lew-Starowicz and anonymous queer readers published in his sex advice column in the progressive student weekly *Itd*, illustrating an early attempt to normalize homosexuality. Karolina Morawska examines the state police's expert discourse on homosexuality and queer subjects' experience of police surveillance, a decades-long effort culminating in Operation Hyacinth.

Part III, "Queer intelligibility and unintelligibility," addresses the paradoxes of (in)visibility and (un)intelligibility of sexually nonconforming women and queer artists. Magdalena Staroszczyk examines the near-absence of a lesbian archive from the People's Republic of Poland and calls on Judith Butler's concept of cultural intelligibility to argue that "lesbian" was a category neither available nor desirable to many non-heteronormative women. Karol Radziszewski and Wojciech Szymański address queer manifestations in Polish visual arts during the mid- to late period of the People's Republic of Poland, juxtaposing the official circulation of artworks to practices originally meant for private consumption or considered amateurish but eventually included in the canon. They focus on three figures: Krzysztof Niemczyk, Krzysztof Jung, and Ryszard Kisiel.

Notes

1 The editors wish to thank Agnieszka Kościańska for her invaluable suggestions regarding the introduction.
2 The weekly *Prawo i Życie* reported on developments regarding homosexuality in the West in the 1960s, as did sex advice columns written by experts in popular weeklies, but there was virtually no public debate on homosexuality in Poland before the mid-1970s (see Basiuk, note 3, in this volume, for a list of some early press articles).

Bibliography

Basiuk, Tomasz. 2000. "'Queerowanie' po polsku." *Furia Pierwsza* 7 (1): 28–36.
Basiuk, Tomasz. 2019. "Od niepisanej umowy milczenia do protopolityczności: dyskursywny i sieciowy charakter społeczności osób homoseksualnych w 'długich latach 70.' w historii mówionej i epistolografii." *Interalia* 14: 28–50.
Borroughs, William. 1993. *Pedał*. Translated by Paweł Lipszyc. Gdańsk: Phantom Press International. [Orig. *Queer*, 1985.]
Boswell, John. 1980. *Christianity, Social Tolerance, and Homosexuality: Gay People in Western Europe from the Beginning of the Christian Era to the Fourteenth Century*. Chicago: University of Chicago Press.
Burszta, Jędrzej. 2019. "'Do czego się było przyznawać, jak nie istniał homoseksualizm?' Różowy język w narracjach pamięci o męskiej homoseksualności w PRL." *Interalia* 14: 7–27.
Cook, Matt, ed. 2007. *A Gay History of Britain: Love and Sex Between Men Since the Middle Ages*. Oxford: Greenwood World Publishing.
Crimp, Douglas. 2012. "*Our Kind of Movies.*" *The Films of Andy Warhol*. Cambridge, MA: MIT Press.
Danbolt, Mathias. 2008. "Front Room—Back Room. An Interview with Douglas Crimp." *Trikster—Nordic Queer Journal* 2. http://trikster.net/2/crimp/5.html.
Fiedotow, Agata. 2012. "Początki ruchu gejowskiego w Polsce przełomu lat osiemdziesiątych i dziewięćdziesiątych XX wieku." In *Kłopoty z seksem w PRL. Rodzenie nie całkiem po ludzku, aborcja, choroby, odmienności*, edited by M. Kula, 241–358. Warszawa: Wyd. Uniwersytetu Warszawskiego.
Foucault, Michel. 1986, Spring. "Of Other Spaces." Translated by Jay Miskowiec. *Diacritics* 16 (1): 22–27.
Garsztecki, Stefan. 2008. "Poland." In *1968 in Europe: A History of Protest and Activism 1956–1977*, edited by Martin Klimke and Joachim Scharloth, 179–187. London: Palgrave Macmillan.
Giza, Jerzy St. 1970. "Wielkomiejskie środowisko homoseksualne—studium kryminologiczne." *Służba MO* 75 (6): 729–744.
Hall, Dorota. 2016. *W poszukiwaniu miejsca. Chrześcijanie LGBT w Polsce*. Warszawa: Wydawnictwo IFiS PAN.
Healey, Dan. 2001. *Homosexual Desire in Revolutionist Russia: The Regulation of Sexual and Gender Dissent*. Chicago and London: The University of Chicago Press.
Hekma, Gert, and Alain Giami, eds. 2014. *Sexual Revolutions*. London: Palgrave Macmillan.
Herzog, Dagmar. 2011. *Sexuality in Europe: A Twentieth-century History*. Cambridge: Cambridge University Press.
Kopka, Sławoj. 1985. "Grupa największego ryzyka." *Prawo i życie* 50.
Kościańska, Agnieszka. 2014. *Płeć, przyjemność i przemoc. Kształtowanie wiedzy eksperckiej o seksualności w Polsce*. Warszawa: Wyd. Uniwersytetu Warszawskiego.
Kościańska, Agnieszka. 2017. *Zobaczyć łosia. Historia polskiej edukacji seksualnej od pierwszej lekcji do internetu*. Wołowiec: Czarne.
Kulpa, Robert, and Joanna Mizielińska, eds. 2016. *De-centring Western Sexualities: Central and Eastern European Perspectives*. London: Routledge.

Kurimay, Anita, and Judit Takács. 2017. "Emergence of the Hungarian Homosexual Movement in Late Refrigerator Socialism." *Sexualities* 20 (5–6): 585–604.

Lišková, Kateřina. 2018. *Sexual Liberation, Socialist Style: Communist Czechoslovakia and the Science of Desire, 1945–1989.* Cambridge: Cambridge University Press.

Majewska, Ewa. 2018. "Public Against Our Will? The Caring Gaze of Leviathan, 'Pink Files' from the 1980s Poland and the Issue of Privacy." *InterAlia* 13: 54–77.

McLellan, Josie. 2011. *Love in the Time of Communism: Intimacy and Sexuality in the GDR.* Cambridge: Cambridge University Press.

Muñoz, José Esteban. 2009. *Cruising Utopia: The Then and There of Queer Futurity.* New York: NYU Press.

Nastulczyk, Tomasz, and Piotr Oczko. 2012. *Homoseksualność staropolska. Przyczynek do badań.* Kraków: Collegium Columbinum.

Niziołek, Grzegorz. 2016. "Coming in. Przyczynek do badania historii homoseksualności." *Teksty Drugie* 6: 282–296.

Nowak, Tomasz Łukasz. 2019. "Przez język ukrycia po słowo na *g*. Kim są bohaterowie czasów *queer before gay*?" *Poznańskie Studia Slawistyczne* 16: 193–208.

O'Dwyer, Connor. 2018. *Coming Out of Communism: The Emergence of LGBT Activism in Eastern Europe.* New York: NYU Press.

Płatek, Monika. 2009. "Sytuacja osób homoseksualnych w prawie karnym." In *Orientacja seksualna i tożsamość płciowa*, edited by Roman Wieruszewski and Mirosław Wyrzykowski, 49–81. Warszawa: Instytut Wydawniczy EuroPrawo.

Ryziński, Remigiusz. 2017. *Foucault w Warszawie.* Warszawa: Wydawnictwo Dowody na Istnienie.

Szcześniak, Magda. 2012. "Queerowanie historii." *Teksty Drugie* 5: 205–223.

Szcześniak, Magda. 2016. "Geje versus pedały. Paradoksy widzialności." In *Normy widzialności. Tożsamość w czasach transformacji*, 158–277. Warszawa: Fundacja Bęc Zmiana.

Szulc, Łukasz. 2012. "From Gay to Queer to Queer.pl: The Names We Dare to Speak in Poland." *Lambda Nordica* 4: 65–98.

Szulc, Łukasz. 2018. *Transnational Homosexuals in Communist Poland: Cross-Border Flows in Gay and Lesbian Magazines.* Cham: Palgrave Macmillan.

Tomasik, Krzysztof. 2012. *Gejerel. Mniejszości seksualne w PRL-u.* Warszawa: Wyd. Krytyki Politycznej.

Warner, Michael. 2002. *Publics and Counterpublics.* New York: Zone Books.

# Part I
Socialities and their literary models

2 Three circles of male homosexual life in state-socialist Poland

Jędrzej Burszta

The chapter examines three circles of male homosexual interaction in socialist Poland, focusing on each one's specific function and the different types of contacts and socialities it enabled. The inspiration for the proposed threefold division came from one of my interview partners. When asked about the social practices of everyday homosexual life in the 1970s, he stated: "You know, the homosexual circles in the People's Republic of Poland, they were really quite hermetic. They were a bit like circles of the inferno." His thought-provoking reference to Dante's *Divine Comedy* pointed to one of the main characteristics of queer sexual cultures in that period—the existence of an unofficial hierarchy of homosexual experience in Poland under socialism, with each of the three circles representing not only different forms of sociality, but also different identifications of queer persons participating in them. Based on a number of oral history interviews, the three circles of male homosexual life were the following: cruising grounds, public bathhouses, and private apartments.

Considering the limited literature and archive on the history of homosexuality in the People's Republic of Poland (see Kurpios 2010; Fiedotow 2012; Tomasik 2018; Szulc 2018), oral history interviews provide an essential source for uncovering and understanding the queer past. I conducted ethnographic interviews with homosexual men focused on their everyday life in the 1970s. The adoption of an oral history perspective allowed me to reconstruct a fragmentary image of queer life, both individual and collective: rooted in the objectively knowable past, in memories brought out during the interviews, in narratives constructed by my interview partners, in their anecdotes, and in significant slippages which occurred during the interviews. Together, these elements complicate the emerging image of the past both for my interview partners and for me as ethnographer.

Before I reconstruct the spatial hierarchy of male homosexual life in socialist Poland, it is necessary to briefly characterize the group of men I had the opportunity to interview. They were self-identified homosexual men, born between 1936 and 1960, with the majority born in the mid-1950s (in the 1970s, they were either adolescents or in their late 20s and early 30s). Although they were born and spent their childhood in various parts of the country, by the 1970s they had either just moved to or had been living in large cities—the majority of them in Warsaw, others in Poznań, Wrocław and Łódź. Most had university degrees. Although they were not "out" as homosexuals in the contemporary understanding of coming out and identity politics—in fact, most of them remain sceptical about the contemporary LGBTQ movement and gay identity—all were active members of different homosexual communities in their respective cities. They "accepted" their homosexuality and lived "a homosexual lifestyle" at a time when this was impossible for many other men and women; thus, their accounts exemplify "success narratives" (see Burszta 2019).[1] They had friends and partners, and they all shared, to some extent, the sense of belonging to a community defined primarily by male same-sex desire. At the same time, their narratives differ in many ways, so that an attempt to organize this diffuse body of memoryscapes perforce leads to omissions, generalizations, and a tendency to emphasize similarities at the cost of differences. What this chapter therefore proposes is a synthetic overview of the social and cultural practices of homosexual men in socialist Poland, organized according to the three "circles of the inferno." Construed as both concept and metaphor, they provoke a reconsideration of what the different experiences tell us about the social reality of pre-emancipatory Poland.

First circle: cruising spaces

The first circle consisted of a myriad cruising grounds located in the public spaces of large cities, and even some smaller towns. Called *pikiety* in Polish, these cruising sites were places adopted by queers for the purpose of engaging in anonymous same-sex acts. Knowledge about the exact location of cruising grounds spread through word-of-mouth but these locations were also situated within specific urban spaces (see Szymański and Radziszewski on Ryszard Kisiel in this volume). Naturally, public cruising spaces were not in any way unique for socialist Poland; it has been argued that male "cruising cultures" are a transhistorical and universal part of the history of male homosexuality (Espinoza 2019, 35–64).[2] The word *pikieta* most often refers to such public spaces as parks, public restrooms (especially in railway stations, at universities), and both indoor and outdoor toilets (the latter called *blaszak* or *grzybek*). Many of my interview partners recall cruising grounds as the place of their first queer experience—if not of engaging in sex with men, then of observing other men express same-sex desire and thereby helping the subjects' self-recognition as homosexual. The act of looking was as important as taking part in the erotic encounter, as some men visited *pikiety* only to observe others, or to pick up a stranger and invite him home. Especially for those who spent their childhood in small towns or villages, moving to a big city—to study or find work—always lead to the discovery of a blooming underground urban homosexual life, and the cruising grounds at parks and restrooms provided a first glimpse into the existence of an otherwise invisible homosexual community. Sneaking into a public restroom and seeing the lustful gazes of other men is often remembered as a major self-defining event in life, a moment of transgression, a realization not only that one is not alone in one's "deviant" desire, but that there are indeed many others just like one, representing every class in society. This experience offered a new insight into one's sexuality, promoting a sense of identity and an intuition of sexual citizenship:

> This alternative model of citizenship is one that cannot be rooted in conventional understandings of public space—or for that matter, private space—but in liminal spaces that disrupt dominant geographies of heterosexuality by creating transitory sites for sexual freedom and pleasure where the immoral is moral and the perverse is normal.
> (Hubbard 2001, 68)

As a specific type of democratic space, and a space that queers the otherwise heteronormative cityspace, these various cruising sites were frequented for various reasons by many different types of men: self-identified homosexuals, like many of my interview partners, but also other men who had sex with men. These included married men looking for a chance to hook up but not identifying as homosexual and young, presumably heterosexual men (called either *żul* or *luj*), offering sex for financial gratification, who sometimes engaged in acts of theft, violence, and even murder. Cruising spaces were also infiltrated by members of the police attempting to monitor the community (see Morawska in this volume).

Laud Humphreys' 1970 *Tearoom Trade: Impersonal Sex in Public Places* is a groundbreaking, if controversial study of cruising in public toilets (referred to as "tea-rooming" in American and "cottaging" in British gay slang). Adopting an ethically questionable methodological approach described as "sociologist-as-*voyeur*" (Humphreys 1970, 16–44), which meant disguising his real identity and posing as a "watchqueen" (a person on the lookout for policemen), this American sociologist acted as a participant observer in a number of public restrooms frequented by men engaging in anonymous sex. Despite its problems, Humphreys' sociological account of the practices, rituals, coded signs, and language characterizing the male homosexuals' "deviant" sexual behaviour was a pioneering study of same-sex desire in urban "queer zones" used for anonymous sex. It showed the specifically urban gay cruising culture, invisible to the majority of society even as it was embedded in public spaces that for brief moments became sites of sexual desire existing and being displayed on the margins, both spatial and temporal, of the city.

While Humphreys focused on the practices and behaviour of men engaging in same-sex acts in cruising areas, I want to highlight another aspect of this circle. Reminiscing on their lives in the 1970s, most of my interview partners refer to *pikiety* as an essential component of homosexual life at that time—one of the few public spaces where they could meet a potential lover, friend, partner. However, very seldom do they view *pikiety* with any kind of nostalgia or romanticism. For many, cruising spaces were a necessary evil, best exemplified by an interview partner's remark: "You have to know one thing: no one ever went to the cruising grounds sober." Indeed, although some acknowledged visiting them frequently to "hunt" for sex, new friends, and even potential long-time partners, others described feeling disgusted, scared, or simply being uninterested in this type of intimate encounter. As one man noted with irony, "boys from good families would never visit public toilets," unintentionally exposing his belief in a class structuring of the three-fold informal hierarchy of homosexual life. Narratives about cruising grounds are often filled with shame, and some men are reluctant to share their stories about cruising because they perceive it as "a thing from the past," not in line with today's gay politics of respectability (see also Król in this volume).[3]

The anonymity connected with this specific public space opened up the possibility of forming intimate relationships with men from all sorts of social or economic backgrounds:

> I have to say, I was rather attracted to these kinds of situations. I liked to pick up a simple guy, you know, a man who would smell of horses and tobacco. . . . Every time I met with a worker or a man from the countryside, well, I was always struck by their inferiority complex. They seemed so lost to me, they had no confidence or belief in themselves.

Cruising sites served the role of literal meeting grounds for homosexually identified individuals who otherwise remained invisible in the public sphere. For younger men, especially those entering the urban homosexual communities, cruising was a rite of initiation. Public cruising spaces provided the possibility of experiencing the universal character of same-sex desire, transgressing the dimensions of class, wealth, education, beliefs, sexual tastes, and so on, even as those differences were sometimes fetishized. Naturally, cruising grounds still function today, sometimes even in the exact same locations. They are arguably not as popular as they were in the past. The absence of an alternative—any other public space in the socialist cityscape that would allow for the expression of same-sex desire—is undoubtedly one of the reasons why many of my interview partners remember them as "primitive," "ugly," "dirty," "humiliating." Despite the often contradictory narratives about the status of *pikiety* in the past and in the present, this circle of homosexual life was nevertheless essential for the formation of larger urban queer communities, as it made same-sex activity between men visible to other men.

Second circle: public bathhouses

The second circle of homosexual erotic and social life in cities were public bathhouses. In Warsaw there were at least three major bathhouses frequented by my interview partners, who refer to them as an "elegant" alternative to the cruising grounds. They describe their architecture in vivid detail, symbolically linking it with the cultures of ancient Greece and thus presenting homosexuality as having a long and respected tradition. They also reconstruct the particular set of coded signs used for negotiating intimate encounters. Similar to cruising grounds, the institution of a public bathhouse can be historically linked with male homosexual communities in different societies; for example, William Peniston notes that these types of public establishments offered some privacy for queer men in nineteenth-century Paris (2011, 9). Although most public bathhouses in the socialist period were open to both genders, on some days of the week they were open exclusively for either women or men. For many city residents who lived in small flats without access to private bathrooms public bathhouses were primarily used for bathing. For others—not only homosexual men—they provided the opportunity for anonymous sex. In most cases, the staff was fully aware of the bathhouse's function as a site for sexual encounters, and they rarely made any problems for the homosexual guests (although they sometimes required a bribe).

I consider the bathhouse a different circle than other cruising spaces for several reasons. First, as some interviewees emphasize, the men who frequented them often belonged to a different, perhaps less diverse group than the men who visited *pikiety*. Because they came there regularly (once, twice a week), they were far less anonymous, making it much easier to develop longer-lasting acquaintances. As a semi-private, semi-public space, bathhouses allowed for a different type of intimacy—striking up a conversation and talking much more freely and openly than in the "straight" world. Although used primarily for sex, they were also a social space that allowed for intergenerational contact between homosexual men of different ages.

My interview partners recounted meeting many "old queens" soaking in the shallow water of the pool who told them stories from their youth. Some shared intimate stories about homosexual life during the Second World War, in Warsaw under Nazi occupation, and even from interwar years. Whether these stories were true or made-up, the encounters provided my interview partners with a sense of shared history. Even if fragmented, subjective, colorized, or told solely for the entertainment of the bathhouse's male audience, this was a shared history of homosexual men and their urban communities from the past, mediated through the queer institution of the bathhouse, itself perceived as a symbolic space embedded in a long, untold history of homosexuality.

The bathhouse represented a more "stable" and multifunctional queer institution than the more ephemeral cruising spaces of public restrooms and parks. In his excellent study of the gentrification reshaping the New York of his youth, *Times Square Red, Times Square Blue* (1999), the American queer writer and theorist Samuel R. Delany wrote about a similar institution—the porn movie houses on New York's 42nd Street. In Delany's account, the porn theatre was an informal institution in which expression of same-sex desire was a means of metonymically experiencing closeness and intimacy with (male) society as a whole, as the blue movies brought together a constellation of different social actors (in terms of race, class, desires, fetishes etc.). The theatre was a unique queer zone created by and among all kinds of men buying a cheap ticket to see a porn flick. Delany acknowledges the significance of these queer counter-institutions when he writes:

> Many gay institutions—clubs, bars of several persuasions, baths, tearoom sex, gay porn movie houses . . . brunches, entertainment, cruising areas, truck stop sex, circuit parties, and many more—have grown up outside the knowledge of much of the straight world. But these institutions have nevertheless grown up very much *within* our society, not outside it.
>
> (Delany 1999, 193–194; emphasis by author)

For Delany, the unofficial institution of a porn theatre is an emblem of a specifically queer way of inhabiting urban space, of expressing same-sex desire and, significantly, of transforming social texture through this desire. His emphasis on the specific type of networking supported by these cruising venues, which enabled inter-class contact and ad hoc alliance-building, offers a new perspective on the social functions of queer spaces where transgressive and "deviant" behaviour occurs. I argue that in socialist-era Poland, the public bathhouse served a similar community-building function in the otherwise "straight" cityscapes. More than only a cruising ground, it represented a symbolic space that revealed the historical "long duration" of homosexuality, even when it was overlooked and ignored.

Third circle: "queer apartment civilization"

The third circle consisted of private apartments. Personal narratives about queer life in the 1970s are filled with colourful stories about private parties and "balls" taking place in the intimate spaces of people's homes. The "privatization" of homosexuality—a result of the almost complete eradication of the topic of homosexuality from public discourse (Tomasik 2018, 19)—led to the emergence of what I propose to call "queer apartment civilization," a secretive male homosexual subculture taking shape on the margins of society and outside the purview of the straight world, in the safe spaces of private homes. Functioning not only as queer spaces, but as alternative cultural and (proto-)political quasi-institutions, these apartments had a fundamental role in the formation of gay urban networks. However, this turn to private space was not unique for queer persons, as it reflects on the general housing deficit which had plagued the People's Republic of Poland since the end of the war. In her essay on Polish "housing culture" (*kultura mieszkania*) Weronika Parfianowicz-Vertun convincingly argues that the entire history of twentieth-century Poland could well be framed as "a history of housing problems":

> Apartments have always been in short supply, their standard generally left a lot to be desired, they were usually overcrowded, and the capricious and intricate policy related to their distribution often resulted in strangers, or people with complicated personal and family relationships, being forced to live together.
>
> (2016, 11)

The scarcity of available apartments, especially for young unmarried people, meant that many were forced to live for many years with their parents, or strangers allocated by the state. For many queer people, the socialist "housing shortage," combined with the virtual non-existence of queer public spaces (e.g. gay neighbourhoods like in the West, or even openly gay bars or restaurants), was especially important for the community-shaping process.

In addition to meeting in their own flats, homosexual men living in large cities often entered a larger gay community, centred around specific apartments. Most of the prominent "gay parlours" (*gejowskie salony*), as they are called by my interview partners, were run by older homosexual men.[4] The owners were often wealthy same-sex couples who belonged to the social and cultural elites of the Polish society. They played the role of hosts of private "balls" held in their homes, and were recognized as the most influential organizers of social life in each community.[5] George Chauncey notes a similar trend in 1930s and 1940s New York City, a time when "apartment parties seemed to be both more common and more significant events in the gay world than in the straight" (1994, 278), which suggests that, in Poland at least, the transnational transmission of gay traditions was perhaps mediated by the West-oriented members of the cultural elite, as well as probably a remnant of a prewar queer practice.[6]

An invitation to one of these private parties was not only an opportunity to socialize with already-known friends and acquaintances—it also provided a much sought-after chance to meet a new partner, perhaps a young newcomer who would have his "debut" at the "ball." But "apartment civilization" served many other roles. It created a safe space for establishing close ties and forming a sense community; or, in fact, many different communities found in almost every large Polish city—my interview partners belonged to different groups which did not necessarily interact with each other at that time. This circle of social contact was the most exclusive and homosocial queer institution. Guests invited to "gay parlours" were recruited mostly among members of elite circles, often intersecting with theatre, show business, and the art world.

The queer apartment civilization had perhaps the most significant influence on the emergence of the post-socialist gay urban community in Poland—and modern Polish gay political identity as such. It was in the spaces of these private apartments that the discourse of "homosexuality as a way of life" first emerged and a shared understanding of "gay culture" was forged. Tomasz Basiuk (2019, 40) writes that gay social life in Polish cities of the 1970s was a crucial factor in the broader discursive transformation around the term "homosexuality" and its cognates, and the emerging sense of homosexual community understood as a community of common fate and shared interests. Participants of this circle engaged in formative cultural practices. Besides partying and socializing together, they exchanged information about gay literature, film, art, and music. Various "queer artefacts" were traded in the safety of the four walls, smuggled mostly from West Germany: homosexual publications (magazines, journals, erotic photographs, and in later years HIV-related pamphlets etc.), pornographic materials (prohibited in socialist Poland), including such cherished rarities as worn-out photocopies of "Tom of Finland" illustrations and early editions of the *Spartacus International Gay Guide*. This small-scale circulation of transnationally exchanged ideas, objects, and knowledges taking place in 1970s Poland, admittedly during a period of relative social liberalization, contradicts the common view that the Communist Bloc was completely isolated from Western (gay) culture (see Szulc 2018 for more on this point). One interview partner shared this story, which illustrates the transcontinental currency of gay icons and the functioning of private parties:

> This guy, P., he lived in Głogowska Street. He ran this great gay parlour. He would organize lavish New Year's Eve parties, for around thirty–forty people from Poznań, mostly elites. P. always performed a kind of karaoke. His most famous performance was Liza Minnelli from *Cabaret*. He had a nice figure, he was a slim boy, perfect, just like Liza. When he dressed up in a costume, with an appropriate wig, you know. . . . And he sang. So, he was famous for it. . . . And later, of course, lots of gossiping all around town [*laughter*]. And then conflicts would arise, naturally, because this one wanted something with that other guy, but she didn't want him, you know, so typical of the community.

As another interview partner summed it up, "under socialism, homosexual life happened mostly in private apartments." Indeed, there were very few public spaces for homosexual men to socialize; although some cities did have gay-friendly cafes and bars, these were in no way similar to underground gay bars functioning at that time, for example in New York or West Berlin. Rather, these establishments only possessed a certain "homosexual aura," welcoming to those in the know, though today they feed a reconstructed myth about Warsaw's homosexual past in particular (see Tomasik, Zabłocki, and Piet 2009, 100–101; Ryziński 2017). Homosexuality as a way of life was relegated solely to the private sphere, and the socialist-era apartment civilization provided a space not only for sociality—although lavish "balls" and more ordinary parties remained at the centre of activity—but also for the forming of a male gay cultural identity, or, more broadly, "a queer way of life."

Conclusions

It is difficult to say to what degree the three circles overlapped. Undoubtedly, there were many homosexual men who practiced midnight cruising in parks and public restrooms while also enjoying the chance to socialize at private parties. The same goes for those who preferred regular visits to the bathhouses, or the few cafes and bars. Indeed, some of my interview partners have shared stories from each circle, while others strongly disavowed having any connection to some of them, citing various reasons.

However, most participated in what I call the queer apartment civilization of the People's Republic of Poland. Some of the most memorable events in their personal narratives is not coming out of the closet (e.g. to family members or colleagues) but coming out into an urban homosexual community. At the same time, this form of socializing—visiting friends for small gatherings in private flats (e.g. for *parapetówka*, a housewarming party organized on the occasion of getting one's own apartment)—was a practice shared by most people in socialist Poland. It can be seen as an expression of traditional Polish hospitability, a cultural pattern cultivated throughout history. Inviting friends over was in many ways a norm in social interactions—but in the case of queer persons, it was also a necessity for those who searched for queer friendship. In fact, the three "circles of the inferno" are presented here in a reversal of Dante's hierarchy. While each of his nine circles gradually increases in wickedness, my interview partners typically recall their first queer encounters as taking place when they were cruising for sex. The cruising grounds and public bathhouses where this would happen were perceived as the more "sinful" spaces, while entry into the private apartment circle and the sense of belonging it produced were experienced as central in the process of their individual self-identification and the forming of a gay male group identity.

Naturally, the three circles did not disappear with the fall of Communism—gay men still engage in cruising in public spaces, and gay saunas can be found in almost every city. But today there are many other circles to join, similarly to there being many different identities for non-heteronormative individuals. However, from the perspective of my interview partners, the three circles reflect an informal hierarchy of gay social life in the 1970s. The division corresponds to a trajectory of queers' self- and group identification as it progressed under state socialism: from self-recognition through the lens of same-sex desire (in cruising spaces), through the discovery of a shared history of social practices (in bathhouses), to participation in the discursive, symbolic and political emergence of a homosexual culture and way of life (in the apartment civilization). The proposed categorization is not merely a reconstruction of a past reality, but also a conceptual framework for reexamining the history of queer sexual cultures in state-socialist Poland. Above all, it demonstrates the different means of shaping queer subjectivities. Whether it was the mutual visibility and shared intimacy offered by cruising sites, the discovery of an intergenerational shared history narrated in the semi-public space of a bathhouse, or the sense of belonging to an emerging queer culture of the apartment civilization, these queer spaces of contact, networking, and socializing promoted the sense of a shared sexual, cultural, and political identity years before the beginning of gay liberation in Poland.

Notes

1 It is important to recognize inherent representational limitations resulting from the specific character of the group of men who agreed to the interviews. Their personal accounts do not—and indeed cannot—paint a complete picture of queer life under state socialism before the first wave of liberation (Warkocki 2014). They tell us nothing about the experiences of queer persons who did not live in large cities and could not enjoy the reassurance and self-identification stemming from a sense of community, of sharing a collective experience of otherness, for example men living in the countryside or in small towns, with few opportunities to express same-sex desire, seek a partner or a friend. They tell us little about the many men who engaged in sporadic anonymous same-sex acts in public parks and restrooms, who longed to lead a homosexual life but, because of social stigma or the invisibility of homosexuality, were compelled to lead double lives as heterosexuals. Most importantly, these narratives fail to address the lives of homosexual women, trans* people and other non-binary queer subjects, since urban gay communities were limited to male gendered bodies.
2 Interestingly, in the Polish language there is no equivalent for the English noun "cruising."
3 In his analysis of *Biuletyn* and *Filo*, the first Polish homosexual *samizdat* publications from the 1980s, Łukasz Szulc traces the discursive process of rejecting the past in order to shape a new political gay identity, one that juxtaposed cruising and anonymous sex with the notion of "romantic love" and "respectability." He notes that in one issue "*Filo* . . . revealed that 80 per cent of the letters that the magazine had received complained about homosexuals cruising for sex in *pikiety*" (Szulc 2018, 200).
4 The term "gay parlours" is used retroactively by interview partners in relation to queer life in the 1970s, since the word "gay" was not yet in use (see Basiuk in this volume). At the time, these private apartments, functioning as "closed cruising grounds," were simply called *salony* (Nowak 2019, 203).
5 The queer urban communities in socialist Poland were almost exclusively male. Women were seldom invited to these private "balls" or parties. One of my interview partners was a heterosexual woman who considered herself part of a homosexual community at that time. A member of the theatre world, she had many gay friends and was often invited to parties. However, all of my interview partners strongly objected when asked if their closest circles consisted also of lesbians or non-heteronormative women. It is fair to assume that in the 1970s the male homosexual communities in Poland remained a separate world and did not interact with lesbian groups (see Staroszczyk in this volume).
6 Interestingly, one of my interview partners claimed that some of the older homosexual men gladly adopted the role of "Gay Mothers"—a reference to the New York underground ballroom culture—by offering assistance to younger men, especially those who experienced financial troubles or were forced out of their homes by their parents.

Bibliography

Basiuk, Tomasz. 2019. "Od niepisanej umowy milczenia do protopolityczności: dyskursywny i sieciowy charakter społeczności osób homoseksualnych w 'długich latach 70.' w historii mówionej i epistolografii." *Interalia* 14: 28–50.

Burszta, Jędrzej. 2019. "'Do czego się było przyznawać, jak nie istniał homoseksualizm?' Różowy język w narracjach pamięci o męskiej homoseksualności w PRL." *Interalia* 14: 7–27.

Chauncey, George. 1994. *New York: Gender, Urban Culture, and the Making of the Gay Male World*. New York: Basic Books.

Delany, Samuel R. 1999. *Times Square Red, Times Square Blue*. New York: New York University Press.

Espinoza, Alex. 2019. *Cruising: An Intimate History of a Radical Pastime*. Los Angeles, CA: The Unnamed Press.

Fiedotow, Agata. 2012. "Początki ruchu gejowskiego w Polsce przełomu lat osiemdziesiątych i dziewięćdziesiątych XX wieku." In *Kłopoty z seksem w PRL. Rodzenie nie całkiem po ludzku, aborcja, choroby, odmienności*, edited by M. Kula, 241–358. Warszawa: Wyd. Uniwersytetu Warszawskiego.

Hubbard, Philip. 2001. "Sex Zones: Intimacy, Citizenship and Public Space." *Sexualities* 4 (1): 51–71.

Humphreys, Laud. 1970. *Tearoom Trade: Impersonal Sex in Public Places*. New Brunswick and London: Aldine Transactions.

Kurpios, Paweł. 2010. "Tożsamość na kartki. Homoseksualiści w PRL." *Dramatika* 3: 30–33.

Nowak, Tomasz Łukasz. 2019. "Przez język ukrycia po słowo na 'g.' Kim są bohaterowie czasów *queer before gay*?" *Poznańskie Studia Polonistyczne* 16: 192–208.

Parfianowicz-Vertun, Weronika. 2016. "Kultura mieszkania. Wstęp." *Kultura Współczesna* 4 (92): 9–14.

Peniston, William A. 2011. *Pederasts and Others: Urban Culture and Sexual Identity in Nineteenth-Century Paris*. New York and London: Routledge.

Ryziński, Remigiusz. 2017. *Foucault w Warszawie*. Warszawa: Wydawnictwo Dowody na Istnienie.

Szulc, Łukasz. 2018. *Transnational Homosexuals in Communist Poland: Cross-Border Flows in Gay and Lesbian Magazines*. Cham: Palgrave Macmillan.

Tomasik, Krzysztof. 2018. *Gejerel*. Warszawa: Wydawnictwo Krytyki Politycznej.

Tomasik, Krzysztof, Krzysztof Zabłocki, and Marcin Piet. 2009. *HomoWarszawa. Przewodnik kulturalno-historyczny*. Warszawa: Abiekt.pl.

Warkocki, Błażej. 2014. "Trzy fale emancypacji homoseksualnej w Polsce." *Porównania* 15: 121–132.

3 One's younger self in personal testimony and literary translation

Tomasz Basiuk

The younger self in my title refers to Eve Kosofsky Sedgwick's contention that queer transformational energy may be mobilized by an interest in one's younger self, an argument she puts forth in a discussion of shame performativity in Henry James (1993b). Such interest is a trope in life writing, motivating self-reflection and the queer self-transformation Sedgwick adumbrates (Basiuk 2013, 163). Her speculation alludes, albeit indirectly, to another essay she published that year, one broaching the matter of the wholesale abandonment of queer youths. This other essay reads in part,

> [t]he presiding asymmetry of value assignment between hetero and homo goes unchallenged everywhere: advice on how to help your kids turn out gay, not to mention your students, your parishioners, your therapy clients, or your military subordinates, is less ubiquitous than you might think.
>
> (Sedgwick 1993a, 161)

Sedgwick thus hints at risks inherent in taking an interest in someone who may seem like a younger version of one's (queer) self. In what follows, I examine two testimonials which partly reflect her preoccupation with this very gesture. In the one instance, such interest becomes the avowed motivation for activism. In the other, the subject's moral agony about intergenerational desire plunges him into an existential crisis.

The first piece of testimony is a letter addressed by one key Polish gay-male activist to another in the 1980s and remarking on James Baldwin's *Giovanni's Room*. The second is an oral history interview with a retired gay man who brings up Henry de Montherlant's *Boys*. It is no coincidence that these literary references are translations. Transnational knowledge transfers played a major role in gay-male identity formation during the closing decades of the People's Republic of Poland (Szulc 2018). Literary translations were part and parcel of that development. Starting in the 1970s, the

Iron Curtain became less impermeable and more people ventured to the West, some never to return, others bringing back impressions and artefacts, including representations of same-sex eroticism and publications about gay activism (pornography of any kind was illegal, but see Radziszewski and Szymański on Krzysztof Jung's acquisition and performative use of pornography in this volume). In the mid-1970s, the future activist Jerzy Krzyszpień spent an academic year in the US and, upon returning, attempted to publish an essay by Frank Kameny which he had translated into the Polish. Failing to find a welcoming press at the time, he only succeeded a decade later.[1] Nonetheless, the pattern of looking Westward is confirmed by others.[2]

Despite the partial silence veiling homosexuality in the People's Republic of Poland, the topic was occasionally addressed in the official press reporting on developments in the West and in a handful of articles about Polish homosexuals.[3] Works of fiction with homoerotic motifs, including literary translations, appeared in print, and films with queer subtexts were sometimes broadcast on public television.[4]

Even sparse allusions to same-sex desire were cherished, as evidenced by letters sent from Poland to the Vienna-based organization Homosexuelle Initiative (HOSI Wien) in the early 1980s. These letters were received and answered, in Polish, by Andrzej Selerowicz, a gay man who had left Poland in 1976, when he was in his late 20s.[5] Selerowicz, who continued to visit Poland for professional reasons and cultivated many friendships there, used the pseudonym Marek Jaworski with his Polish correspondents. Confronted with a growing volume of mail, "Marek" switched to a form letter which became a quarterly newsletter (generically named *Biuletyn*) by 1983 and remained in print until 1987, subsequently adopting the title *Etap* (Szulc 2018, 11). Because access to copying technologies in Poland was restricted by the Soviet-backed regime, the newsletter was printed in Austria and smuggled in batches to Polish distributors, who forwarded copies to regular subscribers. This network was partly modeled on Selerowicz's professional experience in sales and partly on the post-Solidarity underground and its samizdat presses.

Selerowicz's readers supplied recommendations for possible inclusion in the newsletter, such as places to go, films to watch, and press articles and books to read (e.g. *Biuletyn* 1/1986 lists articles about homosexuality and AIDS published in mainstream Polish journals). Correspondents mentioned gay-themed works by Polish authors, such as Rudolf Pankowski, an openly homosexual writer, living and publishing abroad, whose novel *Rudolf* was reissued in Poland in 1984, and a host of literary translations, including Tennessee Williams' *One Arm and Other Stories* (containing the short story "Desire and the Black Masseur"), Manuel Puig's *Kiss of the Spiderwoman*, and Jean Genet's *The Thief's Journal*, all dating from 1984.

Several letters bring up Baldwin's *Another Country*, whose Polish edition of 1968 was reprinted in 1975.[6]

Many letter writers merely mention these and other titles without considering how same-sex relationships are portrayed, implying that any queering representation was precious. One notable exception is Dariusz Prorok, one of Selerowicz's most prominent and prolific correspondents, who comments on Baldwin's *Giovanni's Room*. An activist in his mid-20s, Prorok published an unprecedented piece titled "Jesteśmy inni. Czy homoseksualiści mają prawa?" ("We Are Different. Do Homosexuals Have Rights?") in the officially Communist but quite liberal weekly *Polityka* in November 1985.[7] Using a pseudonym while writing in the first person as a homosexual man, Prorok criticized the then common disrespectful and openly homophobic language. While the word "gay" (Polish: *gej*) was not yet in use, Prorok's defiance arguably made his statement Poland's first gay manifesto. Early in 1986, Selerowicz mentioned Prorok's piece in *Biuletyn*, underscoring that his radicalism was on a par with views being expressed in the West. Apparently at Prorok's request, Selerowicz publicized his real name and postal address.

Prorok's letters to Selerowicz brimmed with activist ideas. He was enthused about the word "gay" and proposed its Polish spelling and declination. He alleged contacts in public television and laid out plans for an underground publishing press, though at a time when homosexual organizing was fledgling, such ambitions must have seemed madcap. One letter, written in January 1986 (mislabelled 1987), just weeks after Prorok's manifesto, was unusually personal in tone. Laying out plans to defect from Poland within a year, he explains his decision by referring to letters sent him care of the weekly *Polityka* and to James Baldwin's *Giovanni's Room*, which he had just read in Selerowicz's translation.[8]

Among the more than 40 letters Prorok received, seven stood out. The writers reminded Prorok of his younger self, prompting him to assert that he was driven by a desire to help such men. The parallel between himself and his imagined avatars is reinforced by that between these unnamed men and Baldwin's fictional character: "I recognized these [letter] writers' great sorrow, their confusion, and their sense of regret. These writers are in their early twenties. It was shocking to see that Giovanni and [they] are so alike."

These identifications are complemented in turn by Prorok's partial identification with these younger men and the fictional Giovanni, as he recalls his first love. In 1975, on first day of secondary school, Prorok was smitten with Krzysztof, a schoolmate three years his senior. After Prorok turned 17, they had an affair which lasted a year and a half and was ended by Krzysztof's conscription and Prorok's temporary move to another city. A few years on, Krzysztof was married with children when Prorok became aware that his former lover sought out men for anonymous sex. This coda to their romance made Prorok doubt that he would ever have a lasting relationship with a same-sex partner if he stayed in Poland. Deciding to emigrate was "an act of self-defence in the face of [impending] spiritual death," a bleak future which Baldwin's novel helped him see and reject.

> I hate this pattern: we meet in some dark corner, jump into bed, then maybe we stay on as a couple. . . . Baldwin has shown me Giovanni and I *will not* end up like him. . . . I am not sure I have successfully communicated to you my disgust with my surroundings, with the way fags here live.
>
> (original emphasis)

Baldwin had already piqued Polish gay readers' interest with depictions of same-sex eroticism in *Another Country*. In *Giovanni's Room*, a first-person narrator named David is confronted with his sexual hypocrisy. Carolyn W. Sylvander calls the novel "melodramatic" (1980, 52) and Velina Manolova reads it as "a tragic narrative" (2017, 131), contending that David's guilt-ridden response to Giovanni's death sentence exemplifies what Raymond Williams calls "liberal tragedy": "the struggle of individual desire, in a false and compromising situation, to break free and know itself" (quoted in Manolova 2017, 147). She points out that "David, in a sense, usurps Giovanni's position as a tragic hero" (148) because Giovanni's fate is controlled by external forces such as racism, class prejudice and, I might add, homophobia—which all play a part in his sentencing—in contrast to David's self-inflicted psychological conflict. David thus embodies "white male liberal guilt" (139), a species of psychological defence mechanism. In this reading, David thinks of Giovanni as an aspect of his own self, simultaneously desired and disavowed.

Manolova's argument would resonate well with the theme of homosexuality, whose spectre David attempts to fend off when abandoning Giovanni. Prorok does not offer a comparably analytical interpretation of the novel, but his letter is structured by a partly analogous web of identifications and disidentifications, not always apparent to him, as he maps his reading onto his memories of Krzysztof, the former love interest now epitomizing hateful hypocrisy—in short, Krzysztof is David to Prorok's Giovanni. And yet, Prorok fails to note how his partial disidentification with Giovanni ("Baldwin has shown me Giovanni and I *will not* end up like him") leads him to unwittingly identify with David. The reversal occurs with Prorok's announced intention of leaving Poland to avoid "spiritual death," an escape plan meant to prevent a tragic end that would be analogous to Giovanni's and which uncannily resembles David's departure for America.

Prorok similarly wavers between his affection for the despondent young men who wrote to him and his reluctant identification with them. They emblematize untainted innocence because, like Giovanni and like Prorok himself, they are rendered powerless by their circumstances. The forced passivity turns them into vicarious erotic objects provoking Prorok's affection, which echoes his affection for his younger self. Prorok thus imagines himself both as a desiring agent in control of his fate, analogous to David and to Krzysztof, and as an immobilized object simultaneously of homophobic harm and of erotic gaze, analogous to Giovanni and to the nameless young men. He presents himself to Selerowicz, his reader in this instance, in those incongruent and even paradoxical guises as a way of justifying his future defection: he is powerless to act but he must act to save himself. Running counter to this complex analogy is the sexual hypocrisy which David and Krzysztof share, but which Prorok aims to avoid. The point here is not to discredit Prorok's activism but to show how the complicated emotion expressed in his letter and motivating his actions is structured by his reading of the novel.

Prorok's enunciation departs from Baldwin's narrative scheme by alluding so clearly to the intergenerational, or pedagogical, model of homosexuality in which the older and more powerful partner assists the younger and inexperienced one. Indeed, this is partly the context for Prorok addressing Selerowicz, who is almost a generation older. In my second and final example, I explore a more troubling manifestation of this pattern by turning to an interview partner who began our conversation by sharing his scepticism about my research, LGBTQ activism and leftist politics. Peter (not his real name) is a former scientist and university professor whose last job before retiring was as a high-ranking bureaucrat. He has remained single his entire life, cherishing this choice because it fostered intellectual growth. Trained in physics, Peter sees himself as a realist who finds the nominalist bias in cultural studies and progressive politics off-putting. While he supports gay rights in principle and appreciates the help which he received from an LGBTQ organization in a personal crisis, he finds the movement's political strategies misguided for being excessively radical and therefore alienating the broader public. Peter specifically disapproves of cross-dressing at pride marches and does not believe that same-sex couples ought to be raising children.

Peter's position regarding the homosexual closet is complicated. Only his younger sister has been told about his homosexuality, yet he insists that other family members have chosen to overlook the truth. At the same time, he seems oblivious to the possibility that his colleagues knew he was homosexual but held their tongue because he never broached the subject with them. Peter's ambivalence about coming out appears motivated by a painful awareness of his attraction to teenage boys. While he had vehemently refused to act on these desires, foregoing a chance to become a schoolteacher, in his middle age he experienced a mental breakdown after falling in love with a 16-year-old boy whom he had been home-schooling at his parents' request. Peter speculates that the pupil awoke in him paternal feelings and invokes the classical concepts of *ephebos* and *erastes*: the theory of homosexuality as pederasty, which he acknowledges intellectually but morally rejects. He is deeply shamed by the thought that the boy may have seen through his feelings, no matter how much Peter wished to hide them.

The agonizing memory is balanced, in Peter's account, by the sexually innocent friendship and assistance he offered a young heterosexual dancer, with whom he has remained close over the years, also after the man started his own family. The principle of self-restraint thus resonates in Peter's personal life, as well as his politics. Peter's account of this friendship illuminates his intellectual perspective on the homosexual closet. Peter moved to Warsaw to attend university. Once there, he socialized with performers and staff of the opera house. In the interview, he underscores the theatre folk's willingness to acknowledge homosexual relationships, which was not the case with the society at large. The theatre was an enclave in which same-sex attraction was treated matter-of-factly, prompting young adepts to be open-minded about sexual variance. (This unique professional community encompassed various demographics, including school-age children who were supernumeraries.) The theatre world was a laboratory of sorts, and Peter posits that its custom of presenting homosexuality as ordinary could be adapted to macroscale. The theatre is thus a closet deconstructing itself and promising a broader social transformation.

Partly contradicting this rational image, Peter fondly recalls a 12-year-old announcing before going on stage that he was dedicating the dance to Peter. He compares the fantasy he entertained that night, of himself as a pharaoh luxuriating in aesthetic pleasure, to his much later professional travels in the Soviet Union, where he was treated like visiting royalty. The memory of the dance is cherished but inappropriate, and Peter expresses embarrassment about indulging in this fantasy, although he does not acknowledge any erotic feelings. He finds a more appropriate articulation of his repudiated eroticism in Henry de Montherlant's *Boys* (*Les Garçons*, 1969), which fictionalizes the writer's experience, in 1912 when he was 16, of being expelled from a Catholic academy for a relationship with another male student.[9] The protagonist develops feelings for a younger and less well-to-do schoolmate. Some of his peers have similar relations with other boys, which the priests simultaneously encourage and censor. Montherlant paints the picture of an epoch passing away as the institution's seemingly exceptional culture is erased after a scandal.

The mention of *Boys* mediates between two major tropes in Peter's testimony. On the one hand, the French academy is another version of the anti-homophobic social laboratory represented by the Warsaw opera house, where same-sex eroticism was acknowledged and could be experienced as positive; it is the (glass) closet reimagined as a model of social change. On the other, Montherlant hardly presents same-sex desire as ordinary, depicting it instead as illicit and thus thrilling. The illicitness is anchored neither in the age difference (with its implication of seduction) nor in same-sex attraction as such; rather, these vectors coincide. *Boys* thus dramatizes Peter's ambivalent stance toward the closet as a place in which illicit sexual desires are secretly harboured and a legitimate safe space in which desire is read as ordinary and which therefore promises an anti-homophobic social transformation.

Giovanni's Room and *Boys* are quite different in their depiction of homosexuality. Although they both present the viewpoint of men whose social standing is higher than their same-sex partners', this power differential receives a critical treatment in Baldwin but a nostalgic one in Montherlant. Prorok's and Peter's readings are nonetheless similar because both entertain fantasies and actual memories of feeling protective about and acting in the interest of younger and less powerful men, in whom they seem to recognize a reflection of their own younger selves. Prorok sees these feelings as motivating his activism, although other motives, including self-interest, are also manifest. Peter sees paternal affection as responsible for one of his enduring friendships and, by implication, a path toward making same-sex eroticism ordinary and therefore accepted. However, tension between altruism and desire is palpable in his account, as Peter seems to deliberately befriend a young dancer who is straight and thus not a potential romantic partner and as he blames his mid-life crisis on paternal feelings capriciously turned erotic.

Both men invoke fictional narratives to express their sense of self-identity and make sense of their personal experience. In doing so, they turn to literary translations available to them in the 1970s and 1980s. The gesture seems typical of the Westward orientation of progressive discourses about homosexuality in the People's Republic of Poland. As it happens, these narrative models reflect, in however different ways, the intergenerational paradigm of homosexuality which Peter locates in ancient Greece before ostensibly rejecting it, and which Prorok acknowledges as altruistic in his assertion of a protective impulse directing him to act in the interest of men, personally unknown to him, who remind him of his younger self. This

30 Tomasz Basiuk

paradigm, one among many identifiable within the spectrum of homosociality defined by Sedgwick (1985) and presenting under different guises, is analogous to the ongoing cultivation of the mostly informal social spaces facilitating encounters among men seeking men and of other queer institutions, also within the theatre and the literary worlds. The cohesive impulses it prompts have helped promote a sense of group identity and transform a proto-political mode of sociability and networking into an imagined community demanding cultural and political self-representation, as confirmed by other interview partners.[10]

Notes

1 Krzyszpień reports sending his translation of Kameny's "Gay is Good" to the weekly *Polityka* following Barbara Pietkiewicz's 1981 reportage "Gorzki fiolet," but meeting with rejection. The gay magazine *Inaczej* published the essay in 1991. Personal communication by email on 24 April 2017.
2 Based on time he spent at universities in Simferopol and Kiev, in Soviet Ukraine, in the late 1970s and early 1980s, an anonymous interview partner remarked that Western lesbian and gay activism provided models for those across the Iron Curtain, who often hoped to emigrate to the West, or at least to St. Petersburg (Leningrad).
3 Notably, by Tadeusz Gorgol, "Homoseksualizm a opinia" in the weekly *Życie Literackie* (1974, no. 17–18), Ewa Pietkiewicz, "Gorzki fiolet" in the weekly *Polityka* (1981, no. 8), Mariusz Szczygieł, "Nie róbcie sensacji" in the weekly *Na przełaj* (1984, no. 38), Dariusz Prorok (as Krzysztof T. Darski), "Jesteśmy inni. Czy homoseksualiści mają prawa?" in *Polityka* (1985, no. 47), Ewa Żychlińska and Mariusz Szczygieł, "Rozgrzeszanie" in *Na przełaj* (1986, no. 51).
4 In my own recollection, a teenage classmate and I discussed bisexuality after we both watched Bob Fosse's *Cabaret* on Polish television in the late 1970s.
5 I am grateful to Kurt Krickler and Anna Szutt for letting me access the collection at HOSI Wien, and to Andrzej Selerowicz for guiding me through it. My information about Selerowicz and his Polish-language newsletter comes from that archive and from several conversations with the man himself. In 1982, just before launching his *Biuletyn*, Selerowicz became head of the Eastern Europe Information Pool (EEIP), established by the International Lesbian and Gay Alliance (ILGA), and in this role he was reporting on the situation of homosexuals in Soviet Bloc countries in a separate English-language newsletter.
6 The openly gay writer Tadeusz Olszewski also recalled reading Baldwin's *Another Country* in translation when interviewed for this project.
7 Prorok's article appeared on 23 November 1985, one week after the infamous Operation Hyacinth had taken place on 16 and 17 November. It is unclear if this timing was coincidental. A man writing to Selerowicz warned him that Prorok, partnered with a male police officer, was an informant. Prorok defected from Poland a year later and went off the grid. (See Morawska in this volume for more on Operation Hyacinth.)
8 Selerowicz, who is a published author today, translated gay-themed fiction. Though his translations were published only post-1989, bound typescripts were

circulating among friends and friends-of-friends during the 1980s, in the manner of samizdat publications.
9 The Polish edition (1973) was presented as Montherlant's utmost achievement, though the novel had been written at the start of his career and remained unpublished for more than four decades. The translator Jacek Trznadel subsequently became an outspoken social conservative. Pierre Sipriot discusses Montherlant's homosexuality in a two-volume biography (Sipriot 1982, 1990).
10 For example, an interview partner recalled that in the early 1990s, when he began to act on his same-sex desires after having been married for some 20 years and raising a child, he offered his services as translator to the newly established gay magazine *Inaczej*. This did not advance his social life, as he never visited the magazine's offices (which were located at a distance from his home) nor met any other contributors. Nonetheless, personal experience told him that his translations would be important to younger gay men.

Bibliography

Baldwin, James. 1975 (1968). *Inny kraj* [*Another Country*, 1962]. Translated by Tadeusz Jan Dehnel and Ludmiła Marjańska (poems), with an afterword by Wacław Sadkowski. Warszawa: PIW.

Baldwin, James. 1991. *Mój Giovanni* [*Giovanni's Room*, 1956]. Translated by Andrzej Selerowicz. Warszawa: PIW.

Basiuk, Tomasz. 2013. *Exposures: American Gay Men's Life Writing Since Stonewall*. Frankfurt: Peter Lang.

Cabaret. 1972. Directed by Bob Fosse. Starring: Liza Minelli, Michael York, Helmut Griem. USA: Allied Artists Pictures and ABC Pictures, Feuer and Martin, Bavaria Film.

de Montherlant, Henry. 1973. *Chłopcy* [*Les Garçons*, 1969]. Translated by Jacek Trznadel. Warszawa: PIW.

Genet, Jean. 1984. *Dziennik złodzieja* [*Journal du voleur*, 1949]. Translated by Piotr Kamiński, with afterword by Jan Prokop. Kraków and Wrocław: Wyd. Literackie.

Manolova, Velina. 2017. "The Tragic 'Complexity of Manhood': Masculinity Formations and Performances in James Baldwin's *Giovanni's Room*." In *Contemporary Masculinities in the UK and the US: Between Bodies and Systems*, edited by Stefan Horlacher and Kevin Floyd. Vol. 16, Global Masculinities series edited by Michael Kimmel and Judith Gardiner, 131–155. Cham: Palgrave Macmillan.

Pankowski, Marian. 1980. *Rudolf*. London: Oficyna Poetów i Malarzy.

Pankowski, Marian. 1984. *Rudolf*. Warszawa: Czytelnik.

Puig, Manuel. 1984. *Pocałunek kobiety Pająka* [*El beso de la mujer araña*, 1976]. Translated by Zofia Wasitowa. Kraków: PIW.

Sedgwick, Eve Kosofsky. 1985. *Between Men: English Literature and Male Homosocial Desire*. New York: Columbia University Press.

Sedgwick, Eve Kosofsky. 1993a. "How to Bring Your Kids Up Gay: The War on Effeminate Boys." Chap. 11 in *Tendencies*. Durham, NC: Duke University Press.

Sedgwick, Eve Kosofsky. 1993b, November. "Queer Performativity: Henry James's *The Art of the Novel*." *GLQ: A Journal of Lesbian and Gay Studies* 1 (1): 1–16.

Sipriot, Pierre. 1990 (1982). *Montherlant sans masque*. Vol. 1 and 2. Paris: Robert Laffont.

Sylvander, Carolyn W. 1980. *James Baldwin*. New York: Frederick Ungar.

Szulc, Łukasz. 2018 (2017). *Transnational Homosexuals in Communist Poland: Cross-Border Flows in Gay and Lesbian Magazines*. Cham: Palgrave Macmillan.

Williams, Tennessee. 1984. *Jednoręki i inne opowiadania* [*One Arm and Other Stories*, 1948]. Translated by Teresa Truszkowska. Kraków: Wyd. Literackie.

4 "Transgression has become a fact"[1]
A Gothic genealogy of queerness in the People's Republic of Poland

Błażej Warkocki

My objective is to note a straightforward fact—one both evident and not—that literary and intellectual life in the People's Republic of Poland had its particular *queer locus*, which was far from clandestine, concealed, or furtive. On the contrary, it has always been well known. Indeed, its status is that of the epistemological *open secret*. That *locus* is the anthology series *Transgresje* (*Transgressions*), peculiar because of its ambiguous generic status and its content. The volumes, which lack introductions, mix original essays with excerpts and translations. The series' queerness lies especially in its centrality to official intellectual culture despite its distinct, minority-inflected focus and subtext. The anthology thus continues the queer tradition of equivocation while setting up a crucial archive and putting forward a localized queer theory. Maria Janion and her collaborators edited the series and oversaw its publication throughout the 1980s, but their work was an offshoot of Janion's seminars held in Gdańsk in the 1970s. The two initial volumes, dating back to the early days of martial law, are perhaps most crucial: *Galernicy wrażliwości* (*Galley Slaves of Sensitivity*, 1981, co-edited with Stanisław Rosiek) and *Odmieńcy* (*Queers*, 1982, co-edited with Zbigniew Majchrowski). The latter volume has since developed something of a cult following, as the word "odmieniec" (queer), previously adopted as a middle name by the transgender modernist poet Piotr Włast (formerly known as Maria Komornicka), has by the late 1990s become a Polish-language term for the primarily US-based queer theory, as proposed by Tomasz Basiuk (2000, 28–36). Further volumes in the series were *Osoby* (*Persons*, 1984, co-edited with Stanisław Rosiek), *Maski* (*Masks*, 2 volumes, 1986, with Stanisław Rosiek), and *Dzieci* (*Children*, 2 volumes, 1988, with Stefan Chwin). The series thus spans seven volumes, each subtextually transgressive and arguably queer in its way.

To discern the queer potential in *Transgresje*, given its considerable clout on the Polish intellectual scene, one must abandon the "totalitarian paradigm" (to use a phrase coined by Małgorzata Fidelis) when thinking of the Communist era. Some authoritarian political systems comprised modernizing and emancipatory projects, as shown in recent studies (Chmielewska, Mrozik, and Wołowiec 2018). Blue-collar women workers have been shown to benefit from emancipation and exert agency in some ways but not in others (Fidelis 2014; Kościańska 2017; Grabowska 2018). While the situation of homosexual persons did not evolve in a direct parallel to the women, it contained a similar contradiction. The Polish criminal law was relatively liberal, even compared to West European states (Szulc 2018, 72–74). The Criminal Code of 1932 (dubbed "Makarewicz's Code") did not criminalize consensual same-sex acts between adults, prostitution excepted until 1969, when the law was amended. However, social oppression and authoritarian persecution of homosexuals were indisputable facts of life, the latter manifesting clearly in the nationwide Operation Hyacinth of 1985, which targeted homosexual men. The social, legal, and political space in which the lives of homosexual persons was lived was thus filled with conflict and contradiction.

The Gothic aesthetic, itself a conflicted and contradictory space, is pertinent when pondering the role of literature in building queer agency and promoting liberation in a homophobic environment. The Gothic is indeed an important focus in *Transgresje*, but also in queer theory more broadly. Eve Kosofsky Sedgwick had an express interest in the Gothic novel since the 1970s, when she worked on her doctoral dissertation, subsequently published as *The Coherence of Gothic Conventions*. Janion focused on the Gothic era in an entirely different cultural and political context, and with somewhat different results. In *Between Men*, Sedgwick offers a deconstructive reading of Freud's study of Paul Daniel Schreber's *Memoirs of My Nervous Illness* to stipulate: "[t]he Gothic novel crystallized for English audiences the terms of a dialectic between male homosexuality and homophobia, in which homophobia appeared thematically in paranoid plots" (1985, 92). The Gothic novel played an important role in conceptualizing homosexuality and, in consequence, in forming the discourse of liberation. However, Poland had neither a discourse of gay liberation nor, as Janion points out, a strong tradition of the Gothic novel in the nineteenth century. That is why Witold Gombrowicz's 1939 novel *Opętani* (translated in 1980 as *Possessed. The Secret of Myslotch*), a mostly forgotten work and his *enfant terrible*, seems so central. Janion juxtaposes Gombrowicz's oeuvre with Jean Genet's intellectual and existential stance in the 1982 volume *Odmieńcy*, a comparison whose intellectual genealogy I retrace.

Janion's first extensive study of Gothicism forms part of her 1972 *Romantyzm, rewolucja, marksizm. Colloquia gdańskie* (*Romanticism, Revolution, Marxism. The Gdańsk Colloquia*). This, her first self-described "mad book" (Szczuka and Janion 2014, 34) is hugely important to her oeuvre. As opposed to her "proper" philological work, Janion thinks of her "mad" books as offering a broader intellectual perspective, and the book on Romanticism became the cornerstone of a vaster intellectual project. It opens with a chapter on Oedipus and Prometheus, who are treated as embodiments of generalized human fate. Gender is not yet an analytical category for Janion, as it would become later. The argument is a perfectly legible, if somewhat indirect, assault on structuralist dogma. Janion contends that criticism is a form of human expression, one closely affiliated with literature. Not reducible to a science or mathematical formula, criticism is itself a kind of literature. The book testifies to the era's openness to Western ideas and forms part of a species of limited "bourgeois revolution" taking place in Poland at the time. (The TV show *Czterdziestolatek* [*Being Forty*], popular in the 1970s, was a popular symptom of this change.)

Janion closes her book with an essay on Gothicism, innocently titled "Zbójcy i upiory" ("Highwaymen and Ghouls"). Her final paragraph offers a clear inkling of her intention:

> I shall consider my work successful if I manage to persuade my readers to accept just one point: what you have read is not, as many may assume, an attempted rehabilitation or renaissance of Gothicism. For one cannot rehabilitate a phenomenon which has a firm presence in modern European consciousness as its integral and inseparable component.
>
> (Janion 1972, 402)

At the time, Janion was reading Gothicism as hinting at the dark side of European modernity. As she recalls in a much later interview, the events of May 1968 in France inspired her. She was aware of the developments there chiefly through magazine subscriptions and books:

> I made friends with people working in a bookshop in Krakowskie Przedmieście [i.e. across from the university], I showed up often to find out what they had in stock, and I would buy stuff. They had *Tel Quel*, among others, and issues of various periodicals would arrive regularly. And the Institute of Literary Research was making extensive acquisitions for its library, periodicals included.
>
> (Szczuka and Janion 2014, 56)

Janion's recollection matters also because the student rebellion of the late 1960s marked the beginning of modern-day gay movement. In *A Tale of Two Utopias. The Political Journey of the Generation of 1968*, Paul Berman (2008) compares East European dissidents to the revolutionary patrons of

New York's Stonewall Inn. It is intriguing that Janion's keen interest in the Gothic originated in this context.

Queer theory's interest in Gothicism may be traced across a massive bibliography. On the most superficial level, this interest is motivated by the seductive aura of decadence and sexual transgression identifiable in classic English Gothic novels, early ones in particular. Janion notes this interest, as in this passage on Matthew Lewis' *The Monk*:

> His intent is to divulge the totality of the blind erotic drive, that single most important master of human nature. This is why the devil seducing Ambrosio first appears as the boy Rosario, to then reveal himself as the girl Matilda. The resulting bizarre turmoil of feelings is reminiscent of the ambiguous amorous entanglements cherished in Baroque-sentimental romances. Leonide mistaken for Calloandro, Calloandro mistaken for Leonide, the precarious troubles of a young man in love with another young man, who is actually a lady, etc. . . . [Mario] Praz, [Tzvetan] Todorov and others list the manifold transformations of desire readily found in so-called fantastic literature (incest, homosexuality, erotic triangles). . . . Nearly all are found in *The Monk*.
>
> (Janion 1972, 380)

Janion discusses the Gothic novel in England and in prewar cinematographic expressionism in Germany. In France, apart from de Sade, whose theory of the novel she examines, Gothicism is present under the guise of surrealism. In Poland, Gothic prose is rare. Other than the mystical Romantic author Juliusz Słowacki, the aristocrat Jan Potocki stands out as the author of *Manuscrit trouvé à Saragosse* (*The Saragossa Manuscript*), written in French, however. A much later writer fits the Gothic bill more easily. Already the publication history of Gombrowicz's *Possessed* is like a Gothic tale, akin to a message found in a bottle. Gombrowicz serialized it under the pen name Z. Niewieski in two dailies (*Dobry Wieczór* and *Kurier Czerwony*), with instalments appearing in 1939 until the outbreak of the war (casting doubts, which were later dispelled, about whether the novel thus appeared in its entirety). The novel was regarded as a failure and fell into oblivion only to resurface after the author's death in 1969, when his place in the literary canon was being debated and *Possessed* was returned to Polish literature (Janion 1975, 167). A crucial step in Gombrowicz's posthumous recognition was a major conference organized by the Institute of Literary Research in April 1975, which resulted in the monumental volume *Gombrowicz i krytycy* (*Gombrowicz and the critics*, 1984).

Possessed was first published under Gombrowicz's name in 1973 as part of his collected works issued by Jerzy Giedroyc in Paris (*Dzieła zebrane*, Vol. 10). Janion deems the novel important and devotes two long essays

"*Transgression has become a fact*" 37

to reading it: "Forma gotycka Gombrowicza" ("Gombrowicz's Gothic Form"), a chapter in her 1975 *Gorączka romantyczna* (*Romantic Fever*), and "'Ciemna' młodość Gombrowicza" ("Gombrowicz's 'Dark' Youth"), a 1980 polemical piece written after the earlier essay triggered a heated dispute in Gombrowicz studies. Reading these essays today, it seems clear that Janion's use of Gombrowicz's self-referential and well-nigh iconic term ("form") in the title of the first essay in combination with the epithet "Gothic," designating a low-brow genre, serves to shore up another suspect linkage, that between Gombrowicz and Jean Genet. Following the publication of Jean-Paul Sartre's *Saint Genet* (1952), Genet has become a blatant symbol of homosexual transgression. With these gestures, Janion introduces the trope of male homosexuality to a reading of the Polish literary canon and, by the same token, adds male homosexuality to the cultural matrix of Poland's collective identity.

Janion's reading had the effect of queering Gothicism, as she pointed to its function as a code for the expression of homosexuality, as well as of homophobia—not unlike Sedgwick. Already in the 1930s, a notorious pamphlet by the critic Ignacy Fik, offensively titled *Literatura choromaniaków* (*Literature of the Sick Maniacs*), referenced both homosexuality and Gothic writings, including Gombrowicz's debut volume of stories, which focus on feelings of being immature. Fik also wrote of "demonocratic literature" (Fik 1961, 126), a term meant to suggest sexual excess. Fik underscores that his coinage is no misprint, but an intentional reference to demons: "the intent behind my etymology is to suggest that this literature has been penned by demons and that these works themselves are crawling with demons" (Fik 1961, 126).

Fik alludes to Gombrowicz in an openly hostile way:

> Should I duly list the key varieties of this sick style, illustrating them with names? Is it not baffling that *these works have been written by people whose maturity came to a standstill at puberty, that they are homosexuals*, exhibitionists and psychopaths, degenerates, drug addicts, individuals with chronic stomach diseases, permanent hospital residents, incapable of telling the difference between waking and sleeping hours, hypochondriacs, neurasthenics, and misanthropes? They write, and they are hailed as great! They exercise their dictatorship! They are perceived as representatives of the present and entrusted with the task of cultural creation.
>
> (Fik 1961, 126; emphasis added)

To complete this illustration of the homophobic uses made of the Gothic, let us note that Alfred Adler opened his book *Das Problem der Homosexualität* (1930, Polish edition: 1935) with a statement about homosexuality rearing its head in the society in semblance of a horrific ghoul. To the literary and the educated, the Gothic rhetoric was a way of addressing homosexuality and of expressing homophobic prejudice. Janion in effect interrupted this game by exposing it.[2] Not surprisingly, Janion's interpretation met with objection. In a 1975 essay "O demonach Gombrowicza" ("On Gombrowicz's Demons"), the eminent critic Jerzy Jarzębski refuses to acknowledge *Possessed* as an important accomplishment, and even less so as a key to Gombrowicz's life and work. Without actually addressing the writer's homosexuality, Jarzębski leaves the impression that the unmentionable "otherness" is paramount. He mocks Janion's hypothesis: "Since direct exposure proves impossible, we are supposed to assume that *Possessed* must reveal some secret truth about Gombrowicz, the kind of truth he would be disinclined to acknowledge in his 'official writings'" (Jarzębski 1975, 4). Indeed, Janion's blending of Gothicism and Gombrowicz's staple "form," announced in her title ("Gombrowicz's Gothic Form"), could not but yield the one result of ushering in a debate on homosexuality both with regard to Gombrowicz and, more broadly, Polish culture.

Janion was not trying to out Gombrowicz in the way Jarzębski presumes, although such attempts had been made before, as in the quoted piece by Fik. Another such attempt, by the renowned critic Artur Sandauer, was made in his 1965 article "Gombrowicz—człowiek i pisarz" ("Gombrowicz— the Man and the Writer"). Yet another, in the excessively malicious and poorly written memoirs by Tadeusz Kępiński (1988), the writer's friend as a youth. By contrast, Janion clearly did not intend to harm or humiliate. Writing about Gombrowicz posthumously, she wished to introduce the once-exorcised queer sexual "demons" to the canon of Polish culture. (Another notable and eminently non-homophobic "outing" of Gombrowicz is accomplished in Plonowska-Ziarek's *Gombrowicz's Grimaces*, 1998.)

The series *Trangresje* is governed by an analogous logic of uncovering repressed or maligned content. In the volume *Odmieńcy* (*Queers*), Janion revisits her linking of Genet and Gombrowicz, and mocks the fear of the "pederast," anticipating Sedgwick's discussion about homosexual panic. Needless to say, Sedgwick's and Janion's political contexts were hardly comparable. Where Sedgwick worked in the tradition of non-separatist feminism, Janion's critical interventions could be read as directed against the authoritarian state or against heteronormativity, or both at once. Her manner of queering Gombrowicz, who had remained deep in the critical closet for decades, was to discuss his work in the context of an essayistic series that itself constituted a species of a queer archive. Without an introduction and containing many literary and non-literary excerpts, *Odmieńcy*, like the other volumes in the series, encouraged readers to read in their own ways. Arguably, the dual reception of *Transgresje* as anti-Communist and as anti-heteronormative continues to the present. Wording on the dust cover flap of the first volume reveals something about what the authors of the series thought of their project:

> We are calling our series *Transgresje* because we have long focused on assorted manifestations—literary, philosophical, biographical, existential—of crossing lines and trespassing boundaries. We have in mind transgression of one's self, of norms, conventions, roles, and socially accepted images—transgression of what is given and formed—by persons wishing to cross "to the other side," to find themselves "beyond the horizon." All too often relegated to the margins as harmless quirkiness, the experience of these "queers" [*odmieńcy*], these "galley slaves of sensitivity," is increasingly being treasured as the unique capital yielded by an inner journey, as proof of fierce defence of one's own individuality, and as a measure of human sensibility in an impersonal technical civilisation, in the face of anonymous science, destruction of the natural environment, the reign of the mediocre and the unremarkable, and the alienation of individuals and communities.

The language of this manifesto is pan-humanist, existentialist, and possibly euphemistic. It is "universalizing" rather than "minoritizing" vis-à-vis queerness, to reference Sedgwick's distinction. Yet, readers picked up on the homosexual question. Reviewing two of the volumes (*Galernicy wrażliwości* and *Odmieńcy*), critic Ryszard Ciemiński drove directly at the thorny matter, revealing that the latter volume contained "sets of texts on Genet," which "leave the door open, though not open wide, to let in another taboo, in effect exposing the book by Janion *et consortes* to flogging by so-called moralists for its alleged dissemination of pornography" (Ciemiński 1982, 9). Indeed, the volumes were harshly attacked in 1982 by *Głos Wybrzeża*, the official press organ of the Regional (Voivodship) Committee of the Polish United Workers' Party. The powers that be thus accused *Odmieńcy* of disseminating pornography and homosexuality (chiefly in relation to the mentions of Genet) and of glorifying insanity (in relation to writings by anti-psychiatrists).

These responses are symptomatic of a political problem Janion was facing when broaching sexuality. Including excerpts from Emma Santos' 1975 *La Malcastrée* (*The Badly Castrated Woman*), she notes, with apparent strategic intent, that Santos was published by a manifestly left-wing French press, which had also printed Karl Marx and Rosa Luxemburg. Janion seems to be addressing the Polish authorities: since the publishers are Marxists and you are Marxists, you should approve of a feminist book. However, the gesture does not simply emphasize Marxism (Janion was a sympathizer) but the mechanisms of power and the concomitant exclusion of the other.

Highlighted in unfavourable reviews, apologetic treatment of insanity was a separate matter. *Galernicy wrażliwości* include excerpts from writings by anti-psychiatrists (Thomas S. Szasz, David Cooper, Christian Delacampagne), who had a broader Polish reception in the 1970s. The role of anti-psychiatry in *Transgresje* was clearly to de-medicalize "existential experience," such as that rendered by Piotr "Odmieniec" Włast/Maria Komornicka, the transgressive modernist poet. The anti-psychiatrists' inclusion is significant because homosexual liberation in the West during the late 1960s and 1970s partly depended on questioning psychiatric, psychological, and psychoanalytic dogmas. (The gesture is emblematized by Guy Hocquenghem's *Homosexual Desire* [1978], polemical toward Freud and subsequently important for queer theory.)

Interviewed by the gay magazine *Inaczej* in February 1997, Janion told the editor Sergiusz Wróblewski about one of her inspirations for the series. The very fact of the interview was significant and transgressive, as in the 1990s the gay press was marginal to Polish public discourse, functioning as a "counterpublic"; perhaps for this reason the interview is missing from Janion's posted biographies. In the interview, Janion spoke about Hans Mayer's *Außenseiter* (1975, translated into English as *Outsiders*; the Polish translation, titled *Odmieńcy*, appeared in 2005). Mayer identifies three "outsiders" of European culture: the woman, the Jew, and the homosexual, focusing on transgression as his point of departure. Janion summarized his argument:

> "Transgression" means crossing the line, transgressing a boundary. Whoever has crossed it finds himself on the outside. Hans Mayer speaks of intentional and of existential transgression. He underscores that the line may be intentionally crossed. . . . But there is also transgression imposed by birth, gender, background, physical or psychological otherness. Such transgression implies another way of crossing the line than does intentional transgression, which arises from an act of will. It implies the presence of a quality beyond the control of its "carrier." In this scenario, Mayer contends, existence itself is transgressive.
> (Wróblewski 1998, 4)

Homosexuality may thus be a form of existential transgression, as it is for Mayer, whose book served as an intellectual inspiration for Janion's *Transgresje*. This raises a question, however. In the series' first two volumes (*Galernicy wrażliwości* and *Odmieńcy*), Mayer's influence is discernible in the focus on the "woman" and the "homosexual." If so, how can the absence of any Jewish theme be explained in any one of the series' volumes? How may we account for this jarring omission? One can only imagine that in post-March 1968, post-pogrom Poland (as described, e.g., by Forecki 2019), Jewish tropes were both excessively traumatic and considerably more politically burdensome than those of homosexuality and of gender identity. Perhaps Janion felt that she was obliged to choose her objectives carefully. Indeed, homosexuality may have been comparatively easier to explore in the late 1970s precisely because it had little recognition and virtually no public or political backing.

One interlocutor interviewed in the CRUSEV study stated simply, "homosexuality did not exist," illustrating its near-unintelligibility (Burszta 2019, 7). No doubt it was truly difficult to be a homosexual under such conditions and recognizing this difficulty can make the significance of *Transgresje* all the more apparent. Any social change must be imagined before it can take place. To paraphrase the historian Michelle Perrot, quoted by Janion in her 1996 *Kobiety i duch inności* (*Women and the Spirit of Otherness*), each revolution is symbolic before becoming structural. Not only is it easier to change words than things, but language and imagination are a dimension of reality (Janion 1996, 70).

Janion renders legible a tradition of speaking of queerness and of the other via debates about Gothicism and especially about Gombrowicz. The 1982 volume *Odmieńcy* is an especially pronounced exposure of this articulation and may even be seen as a step toward enabling positive identification based on an appreciation of the queer/the other. A certain resonating sequence is worth noting: the title and the volume *Odmieńcy* anticipates Krzysztof Darski's 1985 article in the weekly *Polityka*, titled "Jesteśmy inni" ("We Are Different"), a piece usually regarded as an early Polish gay manifesto (though the word "gay" was not yet in use). It also anticipates the title of one of the first gay magazines in Poland, launched in the early 1990s, called *Magazyn Kochających Inaczej* (*Magazine for Those Whose Love Is Different*, later changed to *Inaczej*, i.e., *Different*). Queerness/otherness thus began to serve as an early, euphemistic term for a self-affirmative homosexual identity, before the word gay (spelled "gej" in Polish) came into use at the turn of the 1980s and 1990s.

Transgresje is an archive of queer self-definition and self-knowledge, and hence a profoundly theoretical endeavour which has been somewhat forgotten, displaced in part by the arrival of queer theory, usually from the US, by the late 1990s. This influx and its repercussions have been discussed by others (e.g. Mizielińska and Kulpa 2011; Szulc 2018; O'Dwyer 2018). No doubt that the introduction of queer theory into Polish academic debates helped legitimize queer studies according to the logic of connecting the (semi)peripheries to the centre. Nonetheless, it is worth returning

Notes

1 The phrase is taken from the telling title, magical and performative, of the transcript of a seminar, led by Maria Janion, which took place on 28 June 1979. The seminar was devoted to a translated excerpt from one of Jean Genet's novels. The transcript, titled "Przekroczenie stało się faktem . . ." in the original Polish, was published in *Odmieńcy* (1982, *Queers*), a part of the *Transgresje* (*Transgressions*) series. In addition to questions of translation, the seminar addressed homosexuality as a cultural and existential issue.
2 To give just one additional example of Gothic-inflected homophobia: On the closing pages of his *20 lat literatury polskiej (1919–1938)* (*Twenty Years of Polish Literature [1919–1938]*), Ignacy Fik performs a characteristic exorcism, banishing demons from the domain of Polish literature: "Sexual perversions in the form of homosexuality or lesbian love have acquired the right of citizenship in unexpectedly numerous novels. They are presented very openly and brutally, or else shrouded in a delicate veil of understatement" (Fik 1948, 172).

Bibliography

Adler, Alfred. 1935. *Homoseksualizm. Trening erotyczny i erotyczny odwrót*. Translated by Tadeusz Fajans. Warszawa: Renaissance Ars Medica.
Basiuk, Tomasz. 2000. "'Queerowanie' po polsku." *Furia Pierwsza* 7 (1): 28–36.
Berman, Paul. 2008. *Opowieść o dwóch utopiach. Ewolucja polityczna pokolenia '68*. Translated by Piotr Nowakowski. Kraków: Universitas.
Burszta, Jędrzej. 2019. "'Do czego się było przyznawać, jak nie istniał homoseksualizm?' Różowy język w narracjach pamięci o męskiej homoseksualności w PRL." *Interalia* 14: 7–27.
Chmielewska, Katarzyna, Agnieszka Mrozik, and Grzegorz Wołowiec, eds. 2018. *Komunizm. Idee i praktyki w Polsce 1944–1989*. Warszawa: Wydawnictwo Instytutu Badań literackich PAN.
Ciemiński, Ryszard. 1982. "Alchemia wrażliwości." *Fakty. Tygodnik Społeczno-Kulturalny* 23.
Czterdziestolatek. 1975–1977. Polish TV series directed by Jerzy Gruza.
Darski, Krzysztof [Dariusz Prorok]. 1985, November 23. "Jesteśmy inni: Czy homoseksualiści mają prawa?" *Polityka* 47: 8.
Fidelis, Małgorzata. 2014. *Women, Communism, and Industrialization in Postwar Poland*. Cambridge: Cambridge University Press.
Fik Ignacy. 1948. *20 lat literatury polskiej 1919–1938*. Kraków: „Placówka" Spółdzielnia Pracy i Użytkowników.
Fik Ignacy. 1961. "Literatura choromaniaków." In: *Wybór pism krytycznych*, edited by A. Chruszczyński, 126–135. Warszawa: Książka i Wiedza.
Forecki Piotr. 2019. "Marzec '68 jako pogrom. Brakująca kategoria opisu." In *Tożsamość po pogromie. Świadectwa i interpretacje Marca '68*, edited by A.

"Transgression has become a fact" 43

Mosalik and P. Czapliński, 21–55. Warszawa: Wydawnictwo Instytutu Badań literackich PAN.
Gombrowicz, Witold. 1973. "Opętani. Powieść." In *Varia, tom X*, 211–472. Paris: Instytut Literacki.
Gombrowicz, Witold. 1980. *Possessed, or, the Secret of Myslotch: A Gothic Novel*. Translated by J.A. Underwood. London and Boston: Marion Boyars.
Grabowska, Magdalena. 2018. *Zerwana genealogia. Działalność społeczna i polityczna kobiet po 1945 roku a współczesny polski ruch kobiecy*. Warszawa: Scholar.
Hocquenghem, Guy. 1978. *Homosexual Desire*. Translated by Daniella Dangor, preface Jeffrey Weeks. London: Allison & Busby.
Janion, Maria. 1972. *Romantyzm, rewolucja, marksizm. Colloquia gdańskie*. Gdańsk: Wydawnictwo Gdańskie.
Janion, Maria. 1975. "Forma gotycka Gombrowicza." In *Gorączka romantyczna*, 167–246. Warszawa: PIW.
Janion, Maria. 1980. "'Ciemna' młodość Gombrowicza." *Twórczość* 4: 78–107.
Janion, Maria. 1982. "Przekroczenie stało się faktem (dyskusja nad przekładem „Uroczystości żałobnych" w dniu 28 czerwca 1979 roku)." In *Odmieńcy*, edited by M. Janion and Z. Majchrowski, 285–328. Gdańsk: Wydawnictwo Morskie.
Janion, Maria. 1996. *Kobiety i duch inności*. Warszawa: Wydawnictwo Sic!
Janion, Maria, and Zbigniew Majchrowski, eds. 1982. *Odmieńcy*. Gdańsk: Morskie.
Janion, Maria, and Stanisław Rosiek, eds. 1981. *Galernicy wrażliwości*. Gdańsk: Wydawnictwo Gdańskie.
Jarzębski, Jerzy. 1975. "O demonach Gombrowicza." *Literatura* 28: 4.
Kępiński, Tadeusz. 1988. *Witold Gombrowicz: Studium Portretowe*. Kraków: Wydawnictwo Literackie.
Kościańska, Agnieszka. 2017. *Zobaczyć łosia. Historia polskiej edukacji seksualnej od pierwszej lekcji do internetu*. Wołowiec: Czarne.
Łapiński, Zdzisław, ed. 1984. *Gombrowicz i krytycy*. Kraków: Wydawnictwo Literackie.
Mayer, Hans. 1975. *Außenseiter*. Frankfurt am Main: Suhrkamp Verlag.
Mayer, Hans. 1984. *Outsiders: A Study in Life and Letters*. Translated by Denis M. Sweet. Cambridge, MA: The MIT Press.
Mayer, Hans. 2005. *Odmieńcy*. Translated by Anna Kryczyńska. Warszawa: Wydawnictwo Literackie Muza SA.
Mizielińska, Joanna, and Robert Kulpa, eds. 2011. *De-centring Western Sexualities: Central and Eastern European Perspectives*. Farnham: Ashgate.
O'Dwyer, Conor. 2018. *Coming Out of Communism: The Emergence of LGBT Activism in Eastern Europe*. New York: New York University Press.
Plonowska-Ziarek, Ewa, ed. 1998. *Gombrowicz's Grimaces: Modernism, Gender, Nationality*. Albany: State University of New York Press.
Sandauer, Artur. 1984 (1965). "Witold Gombrowicz—człowiek i dzieło." In *Gombrowicz i krytycy*, edited by Zdzisław Łapiński, 103–127. Kraków: Wydawnictwo Literackie.
Sartre, Jean-Paul. 1952. *Saint Genet. Comédian et Martyr*. Paris: Gallimard.
Sedgwick, Eve Kosofsky. 1985. *Between Men: English Literature and Male Homosocial Desire*. New York: Columbia University Press.

Szczuka, Kazimiera, and Maria Janion. 2014. *Transe—traumy—transgresje*. Warszawa: Wydawnictwo Krytyki Politycznej.

Szulc, Łukasz. 2018. *Transnational Homosexuals in Communist Poland: Cross-Border Flows in Gay and Lesbian Magazines*. Cham: Palgrave Macmillan.

Wróblewski, Sergiusz. 1998. "O wątkach homoerotycznych w literaturze z wybitnym historykiem literatury prof. Marią Janion—rozmawia Sergiusz Wróblewski." *Inaczej* 2: 4–5, 17–18.

5 Queens and faggots, *Petites Folles et Pédales*

Representation of Communist-era Polish queers in translations of *Lubiewo* (*Lovetown*)

Mateusz Wojciech Król

Michał Witkowski's 2004 *Lubiewo* promptly became a transgressive game-changer. It was the first openly queer novel—queer in the anti-assimilationist and rebellious sense of the word—to enter mainstream Polish literature and culture. *Lubiewo* was harshly criticized by some for its shocking themes and aesthetics but most reviewers highlighted its novelty and the promise it brought, comparing it to Boccaccio's *Decameron*.[1] Witkowski cleverly used the turmoil created by these responses. In just one year, he became one of the most popular Polish writers, and—thanks to the effective use of social media—a celebrity appearing on the red carpet at various public occasions. Dominik Antonik commented:

> A new book entered the literary canon and a new personality emerged on the public stage: ostentatiously effeminate/swishy [*przegięty*], breaker of social taboo, politically incorrect, turning extreme vulgarity into literary artistry and wit, eager to reveal the secrets of his trade. The kind of hero Polish culture has been waiting for since the breakthrough in 1989.
>
> (Antonik 2012, 63)

Witkowski's novel has had three successful theatrical adaptations (including at Göteborgs Stadsteater in Sweden) and an audio-book release. It inspired the comic book *Wielki Atlas Ciot Polskich* (*The Great Atlas of Polish Faggots*, 2012). By 2019, it had been translated into 14 languages, including English, French, and German, but also a number of (semi)peripheral languages (e.g. Hungarian, Finnish, Slovenian).[2]

Consisting of two main parts, "The Book of the Street" and "Lewd Beach," *Lubiewo* offers an unprecedented insight into the lives of male homosexuals in state-socialist Poland, juxtaposing the pre-emancipatory, anti-assimilationist queers from the late 1970s and early 1980s with contemporary assimilationist and pro-emancipatory self-identifying gay men. Witkowski used both autobiography and interview-inspired aesthetics to construct his *chef-d'œuvre*. Other contributions to the present volume suggest that interviews with queer people living in those "gray" times are among the best ways to get a glimpse of the queer 1970s behind the Iron Curtain. "The Book of the Street" is constructed as an interview conducted by Witkowski with Patricia and Lucretia, sobriquets of two elderly homosexuals identifying as faggots and queens, invariably speaking in the feminine. Those two colourful characters describe their sexual conquests and other adventures with straight(-ish) men met at cruising spots and with Soviet soldiers outside their military barracks. "The Book of the Street" reflects perfectly the organization of homosexual social life within the three "circles of contact" described by Jędrzej Burszta in this volume: the cruising grounds, whose Polish name recalls the picket line (e.g. the "Cruising Central, "Beaux-Arts," and "Scorched Picket"), the bathhouses (with the famous State Bathing Works in Wrocław where Lucia La Douche was the queen of the house), and the counter-institutions like the Orbis Bar called here "The Little Fairy." "Lewd Beach" is composed of 94 vignettes in which Witkowski introduces a host of other characters. Most are set at the gay nudist beach in Lubiewo on the Baltic coast. A crucial effect in this part of the novel is the juxtaposition of the 1970s queers and the contemporary gay-male activist.

Robert Kulpa and Joanna Mizielińska analyzed the CEE (Central and Eastern Europe) queer social and cultural realities and politics by comparing them to Western sexualities and LGBTQ politics. Their edited volume *De-centring Western Sexualities: Central and Eastern European Perspectives* (2011) is illuminating in this respect. Their analysis of the differences between Western and CEE geotemporalities before and after 1989 can help translators better understand queer realities in Poland then and now. They depict Western geotemporality as a linear "time of sequence," with milestone LGBTQ events/cultural turns occurring in a neatly chronological sequence and helping produce more inclusive and tolerant societies. In another article they state, that:

> [t]he most common narrations of sexual liberation in the West/America, within particular lesbian and gay historiographies, span the homophile days in the 1950s and 1960s, gay liberation in the 1970s, AIDS in the 1980s, and queer times in the 1990s. . . . These narratives were freed from their specific historical and geographic context and became narratives of sexual liberation in general. Moreover, sexual liberation became part of the Western narration of modernity. After the post-communist

revolution, almost over-night, CEE was incorporated into the same historical narrative.

(Kulpa, Mizielińska, and Stasińska 2012, 118)

Łukasz Szulc (2012, 71) highlights that

[i]n the USA, for instance, the narrative of the development of names for sexual minorities goes from queer to gay and back to queer. These name changes mark the progress achieved in both activism (from no activism to assimilationist activism to in-your-face activism) and academia (from no studies to gay and lesbian studies to queer studies). This trajectory often functions as a model for people in other countries as well, again both among activists and academics.

Meanwhile, in the CEE region we should speak rather of the "time of coincidence" with the major LGBTQ milestones being introduced to the mainstream all at once after the fall of the Berlin Wall in 1989. That is why, for instance, the narrative about transgender and bisexual rights entered mainstream discourses in Poland even in the absence of groups or organizations working in this particular field; those concepts were automatically incorporated into the discourse as an imitation of the Western movements and politics (Mizielińska 2011, 92). We face the same problem with queer theories—those concepts were introduced at the same time as the homonormative campaigns calling for gay (and, on a smaller scale, lesbian) emancipation, mainstream visibility, inclusion and (homo)normative sex. The crucial queer concepts and ideas were introduced to Poland by American studies scholars and sociologists who participated in conferences abroad and were more familiar with those topics, which they gradually incorporated into Polish academia (Szulc 2012, 78). Queer paradigms in the Polish LGBTQ NGOs' activities emerged on a larger scale only in the last decade. Kulpa, Mizielińska, and Stasińska (2012, 127–136) note the difficulty with which they function in Polish LGBT organizations, especially the Campaign Against Homophobia.

Why is this context important for translators and translation studies scholars? Why should we delve into the details of Western and CEE geotemporalities when examining non-normative sexualities? Because it helps us better understand the (negative) impact of the hetero- and homonormativities on the translation process and its product. In the past few years, I have analyzed a number of translations of queer texts between Polish, French, and English, trying to understand the theory behind, the strategies, and the praxis of queer translation. I examine here the translations of *Lubiewo* into English (by William Martin) and French (by Madeleine

Nasalik), focusing on those fragments where the impact of hetero- and homonormativities is most visible.

The concept of the homonormativity was introduced by Lisa Duggan in 2003. Homonormativity builds on (neo)liberal politics as it lobbies for the full assimilation of gay and lesbian people into the heteronormative majority. A major postulate of homonormative movements has been their support of gay marriage. By contrast, queer and non(hetero/homo)normative movements are more likely to support non-normative and anti-oppressive relationship models, including polyamory. Homonormativity eschews such "rebellious" queer positions that opt for more freedom and diversity on the level of identity, expression, sexualities, relationships, and politics. Queer scholars and activists may not demand the elimination of sexual identities and labels but they do opt for more diverse and open identity labels; they oppose the exclusion of groups who are weaker, less numerous, and who lack the more powerful tools of gay and lesbian organizations. Non-binary, gender-queer and transgender people, drag queens and kings, people who practice non-normative sex need to fight each day not only against oppressive heteronormativity, but also homonormativity.

Homonormativity is also reflected in the praxis of and the strategies used in translating queer texts. The solutions described in this chapter may have been used consciously or unconsciously. Unconscious use of such a strategy is probably due to the lack of knowledge about queer and gay and lesbian communities, or the lack of appropriate vocabulary; translators may rely on non-normative vocabulary present in the mainstream without delving into the differences (often subtle) between queer and assimilative (gay) discourses.[3] Conscious use of homonormative strategies tends to reduce the radical charge of the source text and adapt it to market expectations, ensuring better readability and greater ease of reception. It may also be politically motivated by the desire to build a "positive image" of queer people.

In looking at the French and the English translations of *Lubiewo*, we can detect two major homonormative strategies:

1 Use of homonormative vocabulary to describe the realities of the queer 1970s—in this case, the translators are using modern, assimilationist, gay vocabulary present globally in the mainstream, instead of the more radical (harder in perception) queer vocabulary (Table 5.1).

The use of terms such as "gay milieu" in the English translation or "le milieu homo" in the French one are great examples of the use of incorrect narrative (modern, post-emancipatory one) to the description of the social organization of homosexuals living in the 1970s in Poland (who may continue to identify themselves as anti-assimilationist or even anti-gay). As

Queens and faggots 49

Table 5.1 Homonormative strategies in queer translation of *Lubiewo*, part 1

Original version	French version	English version
Też tam miałem takiego **kumpla**... nie chodziliśmy że sobą (p. 62) **Blaszak, blaszanka, okrą glak, kipisz** przez pięć dziesiąt lat był dla pedałów czymś w rodzaju dzisiejszego centrum handlowego dla klasy średniej (p. 25) W najprawdziwszym **środowisku pedalskim** (p. 232) Czy moglibyście najpierw powiedzieć mi trochę o **pedalskim** życiu ówczesnego Wrocławia? (p. 17)	Là-bas aussi, tu sais, j'avais un **pote**... on quadrillait séparément (p. 68) Pendant cinquante ans, le **bidon**, également appelé le **bazar, la boîte de conserve, la rotonde**, a représenté pour la communauté homo une espèce de centre commercial (p. 27) Dans le **milieu homo** (p. 245) Pour commencer, est-ce que vous pourriez me décrire un peu **le milieu homo** dans le Wrocław de l'époque? (p. 17)	I even had a **boyfriend** there... we never went out together (p. 62) The **tin, the tin can, the cottage, the tearoom**: for 50 years it did for homos what today's shopping centres do for the middle classes (p. 23) In an entirely **gay milieu** (p. 246) First, perhaps you could tell me something about life for homosexuals in Wrocław back then? (p. 10)

for public toilets used as hook-up grounds, there is a long history and rich vocabulary developed in both French and English languages to describe those places, however none of it was reflected in the translated texts. *Les chapelles, causeuses, ginettes, pagodes,* and *gogues*—these are just some of the names used by Paris homosexuals to describe those toilets. By the decision of City Council of Paris in 1961, all those toilets were transformed from multiple-user (from two to 16 people at a time) into single-user ones as an attempt to "fight against the immoral practices of people using these tabernacles."[4] The normative system was willing to remove those non-normative practices from the public space, and from the language; without proper research on existing queer vocabularies, translators risk reiterating such erasures in their target texts. Another problem is the word "boyfriend" used in the English translation to describe one of the protagonist's friends with whom she never had any romantic or sexual relationship—this choice is not incorrect (apart from "buddy" and "pal," some dictionaries provide "boyfriend" as an equivalent term for "kumpel"), however, "boyfriend" opens up more contemporary and more normative connotations in the readers' minds, which leads to a homonormative characterization of a queer relationship.[5]

50 Mateusz Wojciech Król

Table 5.2 Homonormative strategies in queer translation of *Lubiewo*, part 2

Original version	French version	English version
Podwójny margines, bo raz, że człowiek biedny, a dwa, że **ciota** (p. 91)	On est doublement marginalisés d'abord parce qu'on est pauvre, ensuite parce qu'on est **homo** (p. 99)	Doubly marginal: first, you're poor; second, you're a **poofter** (p. 92)
Nic więc się nie zdziała z lujami hetero, jeśli się że swoim **ciotostwem** ukrywa (p. 282)	Ainsi on n'aboutit à rien si l'on garde secrète sa propre **homosexualité** (p. 310)	With straight grunt it's no use pretending you're not **a queen** (p. 309)
Pedalstwo będzie tak prze źroczyste (p. 210) Wtedy **pedalstwo** to był jeszcze grzech (p. 64)	**L'homosexualité** sera trans parente (p. 214) Car à l'époque **être de la jaquette** était encore considéré comme un péché (pp. 71–72)	**Queerness** will be so trans parent (p. 215) Back in those days **buggery** was still a sin (p. 65)
Choćbyś miał AIDS, już tylko z Tobą chcę (p. 154)	Même **malade du sida**, c'est toi que je veux (p. 158)	You could be **HIV-positive**, I just want to be with you (p. 158)

2   In order to make the text more accessible and more acceptable for the reader, some translators are looking for "lighter" equivalents in their translations (Table 5.2).

Here the non-normative, queer terms *ciota* (faggot) and *ciotostwo/pedalstwo* (faggotry) were translated into the French language with the use of less radical, more palatable terms *homo* and *homosexualité*. Another interesting example from Nasalik's translation is the expression *être de la jaquette* which is a highly literary wording used, for instance, by Marcel Proust. William Martin also used such homonormative solutions, as in his rendering of the phrase "You could even have AIDS" as "You could be HIV-positive." The latter does not reflect the pre-emancipatory realities of Poland in the 1980s and even the 1990s, when common knowledge about HIV/AIDS was scarce. The protagonists are aware of the virus and its deadly effects, but they have no access to, or traffic with, politically correct terminology. The expression "HIV-positive" consequently comes across as homonormative.

At last, I would like to show and comment on some heteronormative strategies used by the translators of *Lubiewo*. I have identified four such strategies in the two translations:

1   Removal of the queer charge. In this strategy, some non-normative/queer fragments, words and styles are entirely removed from the

Queens and faggots 51

translated text. In the examples in Table 5.3, the original protagonists use camp aesthetics to express themselves by speaking in the feminine but normative masculine language/aesthetics is found in the translated texts. The first two examples show this strategy applied by Nasalik, who explicitly changed the grammatical gender in her translation into French. Martin applied the same solution in the third example.

2. Eradicating the queer. I illustrate this strategy with just one example (Table 5.4), where the protagonist Radwanicka is describing her sexual encounter with another man who was urinating on what she describes as her "breasts" (*piersiach*). Martin translates this word as "chest," and

Table 5.3 Heteronormative strategy: removal of the queer load

Original version	French version	English version
Ich zawody, te życiowe i te dla życia: **opiekunka społecz na, salowa, szatniarka** (p. 9) Podają przesłodzoną, letnią herbatę.... Lukrecja zabiera się za podlewanie kwiatków butelką po mleku. Skąd **one** jeszcze ją wytrzasnęły? No i cały czas się **poprawiają, podczesują** (pp. 16–17) W pałacu **margrabiny** de Merteuil (p. 325) Żałuj **Michaśka**, że cię wtedy na świecie nie było (p. 46)	Leur gagne-pain, leur gagne-vie: **assistant social, garçon de salle, préposé au vesti aire** (p. 9) Elles servent un thé léger, trop sucré.... Réglisse se met en tête d'arroser les fleurs, une bouteille de lait en guise d'arrosoir. Où est-ce **qu'il** l'a pêchée, d'ailleurs, cette bouteille? Et sans cesse **ils** se pomponnent, se recoiffent (pp. 16–17) Au château de **la margravine** de Merteuil (p. 343) Quel malheur, **mon petit Michał**, que tu n'aies pas connu cette époque bénie (p. 50)	Their whole lives they made ends meet working as **hostesses, orderlies, cloak-room attendants** (p. 3) They offer me a cup of sweet, lukewarm tea.... Lucretia gets up to water the plants from a Communist-era milk bottle. Who knows where that came from? They preen and primp themselves the whole time (p. 10) In the palace of the **Marquis** de Merteuil (p. 330) What a shame, **Michał**, that you weren't even born (p. 44)

Table 5.4 Heteronormative strategy: use of less radical equivalents

Original version	French version	English version
Szcza po moich **piersiach** i po twarzy. I pluje (p. 248)	Il pisse sur ma **poitrine**, ma figure. Il crache, aussi (p. 273)	Pissing all over my **chest** and face. And spitting on me (p. 271)

Nasalik as "poitrine," thus eliminating the feminizing and sexualizing meaning of the original.[6]

3. Highlighting queerness. This strategy is dangerously close to homo- and transphobic rhetoric as translators use a more radical equivalent compared to the original text. Two examples illustrate this strategy (Table 5.5). While Witkowski is speaking about the sexual harassment of adults in parks, Martin uses "child molesting" (which recalls the common stereotype equating a homosexual with a paedophile). Nasalik introduces in her translation the term "créatures" for "old queens," which makes their otherness more pronounced.

4. Introduction of less vulgar vocabulary (Table 5.6). Slurs and other abusive terms are less vulgar than the ones in the original text. *Cwel* (very submissive bottom) becomes *suceur officiel* in the French version, and *punk* in the English version. *Dziwka bez szkoły* (literally: "whore who didn't complete her schooling") becomes the *pouffiasse analphabète* in French, and *dumb cluck* in English.

The four strategies identified in the two translations of *Lubiewo* are part of a much bigger normalizing phenomenon in queer translation which also

Table 5.5 Heteronormative strategy: highlighting of the queerness

Original version	French version	English version
Gdy nie istniały słowa takie jak „**molestowanie**" (p. 11)	Des temps où n'existaient pas encore des termes tels que "**harcèlement sexuel**" (p. 11)	Back before phrases like "**child molesting**" had been invented (p. 5)
Obserwowałem te **stare cioty** (p. 65)	J'ai observé ces **créatures** d'un autre âge (p. 72)	I would look at those **old queens** (p. 65)

Table 5.6 Heteronormative strategy: introduction of the less vulgar vocabulary

Original version	French version	English version
Im wszystko jedno, ich **cwel** im robi lachę, czy ktoś spoza koszar (p. 47)	Se faire pomper par leur **suceur officiel** à la caserne où par un inconnu, pour eux, ça revenait au même (p. 50)	So it didn't much matter whether it was their **punks** sucking them off or someone from outside the barracks (pp. 45–46)
Ja do niej—„Słuchaj, **dziwko bez szkoły**" (p. 165)	Ecoute, **poufiasse analphabète**! (p. 169)	Listen here, you **dumb cluck** (p. 169)

includes overtly heteronormative strategies. One is the patriarchal privilege of masculinity: patriarchy is at the core of heteronormativity and it is quite visible in the heteronormative strategies in translation (especially in the translation of non-binary and trans narratives), where the male forms of verbs and nouns are being chosen more often than the feminine/queer forms. Another is the medicalization of vocabulary: many translators continue to use such terms as "hermaphrodite," "lesbianism," or "homosexual individual" with their explicitly medical connotations instead of "intersexuality," "lesbian people/women," "gay people/homosexuals," which do not contain this negative load. Yet another is the elimination or the toning down of camp aesthetics: camp has a crucial role in gay/homosexual/queer expression, art, and culture but some translators, consciously or not, diminish or altogether remove camp from their translations.[7]

The homonormative and the heteronormative strategies alike ought to be regarded as anti-models of an ideal queer translation. Translators should be aware of the complexity of the translated queer texts because by inadvertently reproducing negative stereotypes and by introducing normative content they may contribute to the oppression of LGBTQ people by creating unrealistic narratives about them. My goal in analyzing some translations of a key queer text written in Polish has been to build translators' and scholars' awareness of their linguistic choices so that readers may have fuller access to complex and non-normative queer texts.

Notes

1 For example, this review by Dariusz Nowacki, "*Lubiewo* Michała Witkowskiego. Niech o nas czytają," *Gazeta Wyborcza* (3 January 2005), http://wyborcza.pl/1,75517,2475361.html.
2 Information about the published translations of *Lubiewo* comes from the official website of Instytut Książki (a Polish government institution which supports the publishing of work in translation) and is corroborated by a Wikipedia entry on the novel: www.instytutksiazki.pl/autorzy-detal,literatura-polska,1487,witkowski-michal.html and https://pl.wikipedia.org/wiki/Lubiewo_(powiesc).
3 Kulpa's and Mizielińska's analysis of CEE and Western geotemporalities is particularly useful for understanding the simultaneous interrelatedness and distinctiveness of the queer and the lesbian/gay perspectives.
4 See Marc Martin's *Toilettes publiques, histoires privées* and Agnès Giard's "Les Pissotières: paradis perdu?" in *Libération* (1 November 2017, http://sexes.blogs.liberation.fr/2017/11/01/les-pissotieres-paradis-perdu) for more information on the history of homosexuals using public toilets as cruising grounds in Paris in the nineteenth and early twentieth centuries.
5 A similar homonormative strategy was identified by Serena Bassi in "Tick As Appropriate: (a) Gay, (b) Queer, or (c) None of the Above: Translation and Sexual Politics in Lawrence Venuti's *A Hundred Strokes of the Brush Before Bed*." Here Venuti translated the phrase "Mi era sembrato subito **simpatico**" as "He

immediately seemed like a **kindred spirit**," and by doing so—Bassi suggests—the translator refers to the commonly functioning stereotype of the "gay best friend" (Bassi 2014, 311–312) (see also Shugart 2003).

6 B.J. Epstein identifies the strategy of the eradicalization of queer in children's literature (2017).

7 Keith Harvey analyses the contested presence of camp in translation (2012).

Bibliography

Antonik, Dominik. 2012. "Autor jako marka." *Teksty Drugie: teoria literatury, krytyka, interpretacja* 6 (138): 62–76.

Anuradha, Dingwaney, and Carol Maier. 1995. *Between Languages and Cultures.* Pittsburgh: University of Pittsburgh Press.

Bassi, Serena. 2014. "Tick as Appropriate: (a) Gay, (b) Queer, or (c) None of the Above: Translation and Sexual Politics in Lawrence Venuti's *A Hundred Strokes of the Brush Before Bed*." *Comparative Literature Studies* 51 (2), Special Issue: The Gender and Queer Politics of Translation: Literary, Historical, and Cultural Approaches: 298–320.

Bassnett, Susan, and Harish Trivedi. 1999. *Post-Colonial Translation: Theory and Practice.* London: Routledge.

Beatrice, Fischer B., and Matilde Nisbeth Jensen, eds. 2012. *Translation and the Reconfiguration of Power Relations: Revisiting Role and Context of Translation and Interpreting.* Zurich and Berlin: Lit Verlag.

Browne, Kash, and Catherine J. Nasheds, eds. 2016. *Queer Methods and Methodologies: Intersecting Queer Theories and Social Science Research.* London: Routledge.

Burton, William M. 2010. "Inverting the Text: A Proposed Queer Translation Praxis." *In Other Words. Journal for Literary Translators* 36: 54–68.

Conrad, Ryan, ed. 2014. *Against Equality: Queer Revolution, Not Mere Inclusion.* Edinburgh: AK Press.

Crickmar, Marta. 2014. "From Lubiewo to Lovetown: On Translating Camp in Michał Witkowski's Novel into English." In *Redefining Kitsch and Camp in Literature and Culture*, edited by Justyna Stępień, 177–190. Newcastle upon Tyne: Cambridge Scholars Publishing.

Duggan, Lisa. 2003. *The Twilight of Equality: Neoliberalism. Cultural Politics and the Attack on Democracy.* Boston: Beacon Press.

Epstein, B.J. (Brett Jocelyn). 2017. "Eradicalization: Eradicating the Queer in Children's Literature." In *Queer in Translation*, edited by B.J. Epstein and Robert Gillett, 118–128. London: Routledge.

Gramling, David, and Aniruddha Dutta, eds. 2016. Special issue: "Translating Transgender." *Transgender Studies Quarterly* 3 (3–4).

Harvey, Keith. 2000. "Gay Community, Gay Identity, and the Translated Text." *TTR: Traduction, Terminologie, Redaction* 13 (1): 137–165.

Harvey, Keith. 2012. "Translating Camp Talk. Gay Identities and Culture Transfer." In *The Translation Studies Reader*, edited by Lawrence Venuti, 344–364. London: Routledge.

Kulpa, Robert, and Joanna Mizielińska, eds. 2011. *De-centring Western Sexualities: Central and Eastern European Perspectives*. Farnham: Ashgate.
Kulpa, Robert, Joanna Mizielińska, and Agata Stasińska. 2012. "(Un)translatable Queer?, or What Is Lost and Can Be Found in Translation." In *Import—Export—Transport: Queer Theory, Queer Critique and Activism in Motion*, edited by Sushuila Mesquita, Maria Katharina Wiedlack, and Katrin Lasthofer, 115–145. Wien: Zaglossus.
Laszuk, Anna. 2010. "Queer po polsku, czyli nowoczesny closet." *InterAlia* 5: no pagination.
Livia, Anna, and Kira Hall. 1997. *Queerly Phrased: Language, Gender, and Sexuality*. Oxford: Oxford University Press.
Majka, Rafał. 2014. "W ślepym zaułku. Homonormatywność i neoliberalizacja życia społecznego." In *Nowe Studia Kulturowe*, edited by Jacek Kochanowski and Tomasz Wrzosek, 171–188. Warszawa: Wydawnictwo Uniwersytetu Warszawskiego.
Martin, Marc. 2017. *Les Tasses. Toilettes publiques, histoires privées*. Berlin: Agua.
Mizielińska, Joanna. 2011. "Travelling Ideas, Travelling Times: On the Temporalities of LGBT and Queer Politics in Poland and the 'West'." In *De-centring Western Sexualities: Central and Eastern European Perspectives*, edited by Robert Kulpa and Joanna Mizielińska, 85–105. Farnham: Ashgate.
Motschenbacher, Heiko. 2011. "Taking Queer Linguistics Further: Sociolinguistics and Critical Heteronormativity Research." *International Journal of the Sociology of Language* 212: 149–179.
Rejter, Artur. 2013. *Płeć—Język—Kultura*. Katowice: Wydawnictwo Uniwersytetu Śląskiego.
Shugart, Helene A. 2003. "Reinventing Privilege: The New (Gay) Man in Contemporary Popular Media." *Critical Studies in Media Communication* 20 (1): 67–91.
Simon, Sherry. 1996. *Gender in Translation: Cultural Identity and the Politics of Transmission*. London: Routledge.
Snell-Hornby, Mary. 2006. *The Turns of Translation Studies: New Paradigms or Shifting Viewpoints?* Amsterdam: John Benjamins.
Szulc, Łukasz. 2012. "From Queer to Gay to Queer.pl: The Names We Dare to Speak in Poland." *Lambda Nordica* 17 (4): 65–98.
Tymoczko, Maria, and Edwin Gentzler, eds. 2002. *Translation and Power*. Amherst: University of Massachusetts Press.
Witkowski, Michał. 2006. *Lubiewo*. Kraków: Korporacja Ha!art.
Witkowski, Michał. 2007. *Lubiewo*. Translated by Madeleine Nasalik M. Paris: Éditions de l'Olivier.
Witkowski, Michał. 2011. *Lovetown*. Translated by William Martin. London: Portobello Books.
Witkowski, Michał. 2012. *Wielki Atlas Ciot Polskich*. Kraków: Korporacja Ha!art.

Part II
Expert discourses

6 Diagnosing transsexualism, diagnosing society
The blurred genres of Polish sexology in the 1970s and 1980s

Maria Dębińska

The history of medical diagnoses of transsexualism in Poland, as told by its protagonists, starts with a patient's suicide in the early 1960s.[1] Kazimierz Imieliński, the first medical doctor to obtain medical specialization in sexology and founder of the first two sexology clinics in Poland, recalled the event at a meeting of persons diagnosed as transsexual held in Warsaw in 1986:

> The event I am going to relate here was my defeat. A person from Gdańsk came to see us. Transsexual. The case fell to me. My patient manifested high intelligence and sensitivity, making a good first impression. Gradually, I exhausted all ways of helping him that I had at my disposal twenty-five years ago. I did not want to deceive him as there was nothing more I could do. Classical medical approach precluded help. I tried, I trod the paths to specialists I knew among surgeons and others, prompting them to take some action. However, my interventions came to naught. The medical model of the time raised an invisible wall which could not be penetrated. I had to let my patient know I was powerless. And soon I received an unusual letter from Gdańsk—I have kept it to this day—full of beautiful, poetic phrases. My patient informed me that he was committing suicide to draw attention to the problem. With this desperate act he decided to pave the way for others, powerfully signalling to me that I should use his story and his letter in suitable circumstances. He did not directly accuse medicine but between the lines one could read great bitterness. All his hopes and perspectives for a better life came undone. Nobody could help him. This is how he formulated it. And he really did take his own life.
> (Imieliński and Dulko 1989, 68)

The patient who first saw Imieliński in 1959 committed suicide after three years of unsuccessful therapy. The event induced a "quiet and bitter persistence" in Imieliński, who decided to search for ways he could help gender dysphoric persons. He underscored his powerlessness in the early 1960s, when persons who might nowadays identify as transgender or homosexual were treated with electroconvulsive therapy (using Cardiazol), insulin shock therapy, or anti-psychotic drugs used in the treatment of schizophrenia (Largactil), which were supposed to reinforce the effects of psychotherapy (Imieliński 1963, 52). Imieliński spent a big part of his professional life developing other therapy standards, ones that took transgender persons' claims and desires seriously.

In 1964 another encounter took place between a self-diagnosed transsexual woman and a lawyer. The story was related in a light and jocular fashion by the attorney himself during the same meeting:

> One day about twenty years ago I left my attorneys' collective and went home, when the telephone rang.[2] The secretary of the collective informed me that state policemen showed up at the offices looking for a criminal dressed in woman's clothes. I asked that the search be stopped, as an attorneys' collective is protected against it. I got into my car and soon arrived at the office. I explained to the policemen that the law prohibited searching an attorneys' collective offices without a prosecutor's order and I searched on my own. Indeed, in the bathroom there was a scared and weird-looking person. Absolutely ugly, with horrible make-up, in a dress, with skinny legs in high-heeled shoes. As it turned out, this was no criminal.... This was my first client of this type, and quite extraordinary at that. A distinguished musician, winner of international awards. A military officer, married with children. He felt that his psyche was female. For a long time he had been under enormous stress and was looking for a solution to the tragic situation. He was eager to learn about the causes of his condition. Suffice to say that without knowing English he was trying to translate into Polish the essential textbooks on transsexualism; his translations were not very accurate, by the way. In the evenings, he would don female attire and parade in the streets. His wife knew about and tolerated all this. They argued only when he wore her clothes. I decided to take the case.
>
> (Imieliński and Dulko 1989, 295–296)

In 1964, presented with the then available American diagnostic manuals and sexological handbooks as evidence of the plaintiff's transsexualism (before they became standardized in Harry Benjamin's 1966 *Transgender Phenomenon*), a district court in Warsaw decided to rectify her birth certificate. The story was not publicized. After undergoing several gender-confirming surgeries in a hospital near Warsaw, she left Poland. Notably, no surgery was required prior to the legal decision.

Such were the beginnings of sexological and surgical therapy for gender dysphoric persons in Poland: the first legal ruling in favour of a transgender person was made before the medical community recognized transsexualism as a separate disorder. The stories related here testify to the active role of transgender persons in demanding access to surgery and legal recognition. This was achieved in cooperation with sexologists, attorneys, and surgeons. During the next two decades therapeutic procedures were developed that allowed for transition. In 1978 the Polish Supreme Court ruled that legal gender reassignment must be permitted before any irreversible surgeries are performed, using the 1964 case as precedent and reiterating in its opinion the major points made then. The only legal commentary on the 1964 ruling invokes the precepts of socialist humanism as the foundational rule of the state and argues for a humane approach to persons afflicted with such a rare condition: "It is commonly known that sexual abnormality so uncommon as hermaphroditism evokes even in rational persons some strange reflexes of unhealthy curiosity, and especially so called 'terrible burghers'[3] ceaselessly gossip about peculiar neighbours" (Litwin 1965, 602). Therefore, the court was right to take into account not only psychological and biological, but also social aspects of the case: "The moral conflict between the individual and their social environment is a crucial fact in this case and must be treated as a premise of the ruling" (Litwin 1965, 602).

I will argue that from the beginning the state's approach to transgender persons—who were referred to as psychic hermaphrodites, intersexuals, transvestites, or transsexuals before contemporary terminology was adopted—was explicitly a matter of social justice, while the intricacies of medical diagnoses and therapy were left to medical experts. It is important to bear in mind that at the time most Western countries demanded sterilization as a condition of legal gender reassignment and even then, some forbade transgender persons marrying (Sharpe 2002). In Poland, the Supreme Court ruled that such restrictions would constitute an infringement on basic human rights. Gender-confirming surgeries, however, were state-funded for those who decided to pursue them. This progressive legislation was reversed in 1989, three weeks after the first semi-free elections.

This account challenges one of the dichotomies that organize research on LGBT history in the West, namely that between medicalization and emancipation, or, that between normatively understood sexual health and subversive practices that challenge it (Epstein 2003; Eckhert 2016; Spurlin 2019). In describing gender reassignment procedures and sexological therapy of transgender persons in socialist Poland in terms of the mutual influences between the ideology of socialist humanism on the one hand and the sexological theorizations of transsexualism on the other, I demonstrate that medicalization of LGBT experiences and desires had radically different effects under state socialism. Without claiming that the critiques of medicalization in Western capitalist countries are misaimed or flawed, I take issue with their application outside the context of the social struggles from which they emerged. I argue that the state-socialist context produced a different configuration of social actors and power relations, one in which medicalization enabled social and political advocacy for transgender persons' rights.

Modern dichotomies

My argument is offered in the context of current debates on the history of women's and sexual minorities' organizing under state socialism by the so-called Revisionist Feminist Scholars (Funk 2014) rediscovering the history of women's agency in the Eastern Bloc (Fidelis 2010; de Haan 2010; Grabowska 2012; Ghodsee 2014, 2019) and scholars of gay and lesbian history critiquing the renderings of LGBT history in Eastern Europe that cast it against the history of LGBT organizing in the West that serves as a norm and a path for others to follow (Renkin 2009, 2016; Kulpa and Mizielińska 2016; Szulc 2018). This scholarship has a double aim: it recovers histories that have been silenced in transition to liberal democracy and capitalism in post-socialist countries and, by doing so, it challenges the underlying assumptions and conceptual frameworks of Western scholarship on women's and LGBT activism in Central and Eastern Europe. This chapter adds a transgender perspective to this body of scholarship: it reconstructs the state-socialist concept of transsexualism and the activities of the "therapeutic community" formed by sexologists and their patients to argue for a more nuanced concept of medicalization, one that could account for the experiences and practices concerning transgender persons in socialist Poland.

However, before embarking on this task I would like to engage the available "revisionist" literature on women and gays under state socialism, exploring the threads that relate to my own research, namely, the loaded character of the metaphor of Iron Curtain and the essentializing of societies behind it; the instant erasure of women's and LGBT activism in 1989 and the self-orientalizing discourses of women and gay activists after 1989; the recognition that some common social science concepts—the distinctions between structure and agency, state and grassroots activism, Western time of progress and Eastern stagnation and traditionalism—have their source in the political rhetoric of the Cold War.

The widespread use of the metaphor of the Iron Curtain has contributed to the orientalization of socialist countries. In the words of Francesca de Haan:

> During the Cold War, this West–East (positive–negative, light–dark) binary pivoted around the metaphor of the Iron Curtain, which in the western hegemonic view separated "the free West" from its dark,

homogenised Other, "the Soviet block" [sic], or an oppressed "Eastern Europe," characterised by everything it supposedly lacked (Christian civilisation, freedom, civil society, feminism . . .).

(de Haan 2010, 556)

The metaphor suggests impermeability of the border between Eastern and Western Blocs and impenetrability of state-socialist countries—an absolute lack of contact and exchange across the border. Recent scholarship reveals that this imagery served a certain political rhetoric but had little to do with reality. Despite restrictions on individual travel and exchange of ideas due to censorship, there were wide international networks of women active in women's organizations who participated in the UN Decade for Women (1975–1985), a series of international conferences that developed the international women's movement. Moreover, according to Kristen Ghodsee, socialist women in coalition with the women from what was then called the third world set the tone of those UN conferences and were key actors in defining the goals of global women's activism of that era, while American women had to manoeuvre a difficult political situation at home and be cautious in interactions with socialist or third world women:

> The accusations of rightwing politicians that American feminists must be communists, and the FBI infiltration of domestic women's organizations had a chilling effect on women's rights advocates. Prudent American women kept safely apart from their counterparts in the Eastern Bloc.
>
> (Ghodsee 2019, 14)

Ghodsee goes so far as to say that pro-women activities of the American administration at the time were a reaction to the initiatives of leftist women's organizations both at home and abroad. This contradicts and reverts the common image of women from socialist countries as puppets, blindly pursuing the agenda provided by their governments.

As women's activists engaged in intellectual and political exchanges on the ground of international UN conferences, gays from some countries in the Eastern Bloc had their own networks of contacts on the other side of the Iron Curtain, as Łukasz Szulc recently demonstrated by analyzing underground gay magazines from the 1980s (Szulc 2018). Szulc describes the process of forming a gay public in socialist Poland, and to a lesser extent in East Germany (GDR), underscoring contacts between Western and Eastern activists. While Western activists were trying to encourage Eastern homosexuals to establish organizations and undertake Western-style political activities, they met with reluctance or indifference. Szulc quotes one of the early reports: "In those countries where a certain amount of liberation prevails, e.g., Hungary and Poland, homosexuals are content with their present freedom and lifestyle, e.g., private parties and nude beaches, and do not want to endanger it by unnecessary manifestos" (EEIP 1983, 2, quoted in Szulc 2018, 63). However, both in Poland and the GDR there were gay organizations, such as the working group "Homosexuals in the Church" organized by the Evangelical Church in East Germany, whose members were critical of the EEIP (Eastern European Information Pool) publications for their anti-Communist bias:

> A distinct anti-communist prejudice stretches through almost all of the articles. Even some of the well-meant articles get caught up in the twilight of a political statement that cannot be accepted by us. . . . To put it plainly: We lesbians and gay men from the Church working groups of the GDR are basically endeavouring to win sympathy from our society and its socialistic order. . . . All problems concerning us can only be solved in our context of government or not at all.
> (EEIP 1985, 4, quoted in Szulc 2018, 69)

According to Szulc, the local critics of the "saving gays narrative" that characterized Western activists' approach to Eastern Europe pointed out that legislation in some Eastern Bloc countries, such as GDR, was more progressive than in many Western countries at that time. In Poland, too, the state's attitude towards homosexual persons was ambiguous. On the one hand, there was persecution by secret police, on the other, the legislation was more liberal than in many Western countries and the state supported certain local and international activities, going so far as to make party premises available for local and international activist meetings (Szulc 2018, 213). Therefore, gay activists in Poland, Hungary, and East Germany, while closely cooperating with Western LGBT organizations such as ILGA, were also able to find allies in the local state structures and criticize the orientalizing discourses that dominated Western activism at the time. The same can be said about socialist women, whose contacts with Western feminists at UN conferences resulted in the articulation of different goals, political views, and understandings of women's rights (Ghodsee 2019, 19).

After 1989 in Poland the forms of activism afforded by the socialist state were immediately delegitimized and erased from public memory, and the progressive legislation of the previous period reversed. Abortion was banned, the right to strike severely limited, while the legal gender reassignment procedure was first abolished and then reintroduced in the form of a long, complicated, and humiliating court trial. State funding for gender-confirming surgeries was withdrawn after the healthcare system reform in

1999. At the same time and, I would like to argue, due to those erasures in political, social scientific, and activist discourses, Poland and other Eastern European countries were being constructed as backward and in need of catching up with the West. Hadley Renkin argues that the discourses of Eastern European homophobia are a technology for making geographical and political demarcations: "LGBT people appear here as a kind of 'indicator species' for the postsocialist creation of inclusive society—for 'normal' social progress" (Renkin 2009, 25). Thus, the efforts to improve the social and legal situation of LGBT persons in Poland have been wrapped in the self-orientalizing rhetoric of modernization and returning to the West: "homophobia came to signal not merely personal psychological failure, but a wider failure of the capacity for reason and civilization—and to stand as a particularly resonant sign of the failed modern, civilized, tolerant European self" (Renkin 2016, 180).

The same could be said for the struggle over women's rights: the conviction that socialist women's activism cannot be counted as feminism persisted throughout the 1990s, while Polish feminists embraced this self-orientalizing narrative and worked to adopt Western forms of social activism, even as they acknowledged that socialist legislation was in many respects more progressive than its Western counterparts (Grabowska 2012, 2018). This new activism usually took the form of nongovernmental organizations using the slogans of building civil society, democratization, and Europeanization (Grabowska 2012; Załęski 2012). Similarly, the hegemonic character of Western LGBT historiography posits the history of LGBT movements in the USA as the only viable path to liberation that other regions should follow. However, as pointed out by Joanna Mizielińska, the timelines of Western and Eastern LGBT history are incommensurate (Mizielińska 2016) and the various narratives and strategies developed as a consequence of one another in the West were all adapted simultaneously in Poland after 1989.

Ghodsee points out that Western social science regarding social movements was based on dichotomies that guided the Cold War political rhetoric: grassroots movements vs. the state, structure vs. agency, the Western history of progress and liberation vs. the Eastern history of traditionalism and oppression. She claims that "[t]he ongoing fetishization of nonstate actors is rooted in a Cold War bias against state-based solutions to social problems" (Ghodsee 2014, 561). This rhetoric, combined with the erasure of progressive socialist policies after 1989, has had an impact on the activist and social science vocabularies. Concepts of political agency dominant in Western sociology universalize local histories and political strategies by projecting them onto Central and Eastern European contexts while their roots in particular histories and geographies of social activism become obscured. Thus, no longer seen as political tools, they are turned into objective social scientific categories.

Sexology as sociology

For the reasons explored in the previous section, the history of the legal and medical gender reassignment procedure before 1989 has also been erased and forgotten. I use sexological literature of the time and the occasional papers published by sexologists in legal journals to recreate the major tenets of the practice and to expound the vision of the relationship between the transgender individual and the society they propose. This allows me to analyze the meaning and effects of medicalization of transgender experiences under state socialism.

The emergence of terminology and diagnostic procedure concerning transgender persons in Poland was a process analogous to the development of diagnostic standards in the USA (Benjamin 1966; Meyerowitz 1980). An exchange of ideas was in place. For example, Stanisław Dulko, Imieliński's most prominent follower who continues to advocate for transgender rights, studied under John Money at Johns Hopkins University on a Fulbright Scholarship.[4] However, the approach of Polish sexologists towards diagnosis and treatment of persons who demanded gender reassignment was as much influenced by Western science as by the domestic context, such as the state-funded healthcare system and the official ideology of socialist humanism.

The particular history of Polish sexology after Second World War is described by Agnieszka Kościańska (2014). Poland was one of the few countries where sexology constituted a separate medical specialization. Imieliński, its founder, not only worked to establish the first two sexology clinics, but was also a tireless popularizer of sexological knowledge, cooperating with lawyers and humanities scholars to promote his humanistic vision of human sexuality (Imieliński 1980). According to Kościańska and contrary to stereotypical images of the prudish socialist state, sexual pleasure, gender roles, contraception, and sexual hygiene were important topics of public discussion before 1989. However, they were framed in terms of sexual education rather than liberation. The revolutionary fervour that characterized German sexology in the 1920s or postwar American sexology was absent from Poland, where the positivistic impulse to enlighten the masses prevailed.

The fact that sexology in Poland favoured a holistic approach to sexuality, emphasizing psychotherapy and the building of intimate relationships in contrast to Western research on the mechanics of orgasm and the invention of Viagra, was due not only to a lack of money or to socialist prudishness, but most of all to the critique of commercialized sexuality associated with the West (Kościańska 2014, 66). Polish sexology had the ambition to be a tool of social critique and change, an approach firmly rooted in the tradition of the nineteenth-century Polish intelligentsia. For this project, "Western culture" became an important but negative point of reference. A spectacular example is an entry in Imieliński's encyclopaedia of sexology defining the "Western culture syndrome." I abbreviate his long and dense definition for clarity:

> The syndrome develops in the cultural context of Western industrial societies and the social changes they are undergoing. It comprises of several symptoms: 1) obsessive focus on the end result of intercourse without being able to concentrate on the process, which results in shortened time of sexual activity and lack of emotional satisfaction; 2) focus on developing the technical aspects of intercourse instead of intensifying emotional experience; 3) discrepancy between informational and emotional aspects of sexual experience—positive intellectual opinion of sexuality combines with emotional depreciation or hostility; 4) sexual intolerance—diversity of sexual experience is a source of fear, hostility and repression. The syndrome results in lack of emotional satisfaction from sexual intercourse, higher proclivity towards sexual dysfunction and difficulties in developing deep bonds with sexual partners.
> (Imieliński 1985, 440)

Here, sexological diagnosis is a purely social diagnosis, as it is difficult to imagine anyone being diagnosed with this syndrome. Sexuality is not a function of biology but an integral part of individual and social life. Social and psychological aspects are crucial for Imieliński, as he downplays issues of physiology and dismisses sex toys as "prostheses."

Treating sexual intolerance as a symptom of disorder was consistent with the approach to gender dysphoric patients developed by Imieliński and his students. When it came to patients who today might call themselves transgender, the official doctrine of socialist humanism allowed sexologists to introduce a humanistic model of medicine prioritizing measures aimed at easing the pain of transgender persons and focused on their wellbeing. Thus, the procedure afforded transgender patients areas of freedom other than the medico-legal practices common in the West at the time.

Legal gender reassignment as therapy

The 1978 ruling was published with two commentaries, one of which was authored by Imieliński and Dulko (Polish Supreme Court 1983). After explaining the medical understanding of transsexualism at the time, they recommend allowing rectification for transsexuals and in "special cases of homosexuals and transvestites" (Polish Supreme Court 1983, 515). They argue that legal gender reassignment has therapeutic effects even if it is not followed by gender affirming surgeries, which cause ethical concerns among surgeons and entail the risk of failure. Therefore, surgical interventions should be undertaken only when the sole rectification of the birth certificate does not bring satisfactory therapeutic results. The proposition to allow gender reassignment also in particular (but unspecified) cases of homosexuality and transvestism, which may sound as gravely pathologizing homosexuality, should rather be read as an attempt to allow gender reassignment also in cases that do not match the strict diagnostic criteria of transsexualism.

Sexologists publishing in legal journals is meaningful in and of itself, especially that a few years later lawyers opposing the ruling would themselves undertake to explain biological facts and formulate definitions of gender. The sexologists' commentaries from the early 1980s underscored that the basic criterion for assessing a patient's gender should be their self-identification. The importance of surgery is downplayed in these early commentaries but other papers describe successful transitions in which gender-confirming surgeries allowed for a happy marital life (Dulko 1982). One paper reports the case of a transsexual man who had forged his documents to get married and was brought to court upon the discovery of his crime. Provided with a sexological diagnosis of his transsexualism, the court decided not to punish him but to rectify his documents instead (Imieliński, Dulko, and Czernikiewicz 1983). Apparently, the focus of sexologists' arguments was the wellbeing of their patient and not proper diagnostic differentiation. The boundaries between the biological and the social aspects of transsexualism seem purposefully blurred. Strikingly, in the grim period of martial law and political persecution, judges were extremely favourable towards transgender persons.

Public sociology

Apart from numerous papers in legal and medical journals, Imieliński and Dulko authored popular books touching on transsexualism and gender dysphoria. Two were published in the late 1980s: *Przekleństwo Androgyne* (*The Curse of Androgyne*) in 1988 and *Apokalipsa płci* (*Gender Apocalypse*) in 1989 (Imieliński and Dulko 1988, 1989). The former, a popularizing treatise on transsexualism and, to a lesser extent, transvestism and homosexuality, their aetiology and therapy, makes a plea for tolerance and understanding. The latter is a collection of memoirs, poems, autobiographic accounts, and records of discussions held at the sexology clinic in Warsaw in the 1980s which gives voice to transgender persons themselves. While the collection was curated by the editors, who declare that they chose the most typical and representative accounts, these are written in the first person and describe the everyday trials and tribulations of transgender persons, providing a glimpse of the local sociology of gender.

Both publications are premised upon the holistic vision that does not make a sharp distinction between society and biology, between social ills and medical diseases. *Przekleństwo Androgyne* ends with the following diagnosis:

> "Queers should be castrated or put in an asylum"—so argue various "Catos." We pity those specimens, because they do not know that they themselves are sick. From hate. From repression and insecurities. From deficient humanity. Intolerant society shapes two syndromes: the disease of rebellion against restrictive norms (those rebels are called deviants) and the disease of conforming to those norms, which affects many of us (those calling every difference a deviance). But maladjusted persons may be more worthy [sic] than "normal" persons. The existence of otherness signals the relativity of our ways of thinking and teaches us humility before the richness and complexity of reality.
>
> (Imieliński and Dulko 1988, 271)

These popular books can be interpreted as an attempt at therapy: the society needs to be cured from intolerance as much as transgender people need help in the form of legal gender reassignment, hormones, and surgeries. Pathology is defined as the loneliness and suffering of transgender persons and not their medical needs. Time and again sexologists use medical language to articulate moral and social diagnoses and to advocate for change in societal attitudes towards their patients.

The two volumes thus aimed at creating, or rather, widening the public for transgender stories. Education was supposed to be achieved through compassion and understanding for the experiences of transgender persons. The autobiographies, poems, and memoirs describe a hostile social environment: violence experienced from parents and peers, indifference on the part of psychologists and other medical specialists. They contain many love stories, which are there to prove that transgender persons are able to engage in deeply intimate relationships. Unfortunately, these stories often utilize negative stereotypes about homosexual persons. The accounts further addressed transgender persons in need of gender reassignment by providing information on the process of therapy and an insight into the experiences of those who had undergone transition. They were a product of a "therapeutic community" that sexologists tried to build around the sexology clinic in Warsaw by organizing meetings for patients and their partners and families, as well as experts such as surgeons, lawyers, and priests (the clinic employed a priest as spiritual support for the patients). This was a space in which to share individual experiences but also discuss the social situation of transgender persons: their fears and desires regarding their social environment. The community was one of the sites where social diagnoses and strategies to advocate for transgender rights emerged.

Exclusions

Expanding the category of disease to include conformism and intolerance was a rhetorical device aimed to depathologize transsexualism. The use of medical vocabulary in this context did not pathologize gender nonconforming individuals but strengthened the social critique addressed at intolerant society. However, the strategy had a downside: the humanistic approach to transsexualism was presented as only rational and in accordance with nature at the cost of stark heteronormativity. Though the effect may not have been intended, humanistic sexology reinforced the sexual hierarchy identified by Gayle Rubin (2011). In another publication Imieliński underscores that "so much as treating a sexual deviation as an illness that has to be 'diagnosed' may cause trauma, especially because such diagnoses typically entail some element of moral condemnation and social opprobrium" (Imieliński 1990, 2:49). Nonetheless, a discursive effect of the literature on transsexualism was further pathologization of homosexuality, which was implicitly presented as something worse than a medical condition. Transsexualism at least could be cured, and it is clear from the sexological publications discussed here that in the 1980s it seemed less shameful and more "natural" than homosexuality.

Conclusions

The transition from medicalized to liberated sexual identities is an element of the Western "timeline of consequence" (Mizielińska 2016). In Poland, however, the medical category of transsexualism as an inborn psychological condition helped provide transgender persons with the most liberal conditions for legal gender reassignment imaginable at the time. The language of medicine and therapy was used to argue that legal recognition was a condition of individual health, and that intolerant society needed therapy. Medicalization allowed the therapeutic community to arise under political circumstances that did not allow freedom of association and to demand legal and social justice for transgender persons. The all-encompassing medical language of Polish sexology did not maintain the nature-culture divide but allowed sexologists to articulate sociological diagnoses and advocate for more tolerance towards their patients. The current concept of medicalization fails to convey the complexity and ambiguity of this phenomenon.

Regarding the "revisionist history" of women's and LGBT emancipation under state socialism, the modernizing impulse of the 1990s that institutionalized women's and LGBT activism in the form of nongovernmental organizations and introduced Western-style activist strategies and agendas resulted from the erasure of a different kind of modernization: the socialist one. As Michel-Rolph Trouillot (2002) powerfully demonstrates, the Western and the modern are always constituted through and against a nonmodern Other. Such has been the place of Eastern Europe in the political and scientific discourses on women's liberation and sexual citizenship, a region coded as traditionalist, homophobic, and patriarchal. However, Trouillot goes on to describe another type of Other—one found within modernity itself:

> I have argued so far that modernity is structurally plural inasmuch as it requires an heterology, an Other outside of itself. I would like to argue now that the modern is also historically plural because it always requires an Other from within, the otherwise modern, created between the jaws of modernity and modernization.
>
> (Trouillot 2002, 228)

The project of socialist humanism in Polish sexology and the resulting standards of treatment of transgender persons may be regarded as an alternative modernity, one in which the same building blocks—the modern dichotomies between sex and gender, soma and psyche, nature and culture, individual and society (Latour 1993)—are used to construct an entirely different building.

Acknowledgement

This chapter is based on doctoral research conducted in the years 2009–2013 at the Graduate School for Social Research, Polish Academy of Sciences, and in 2013–2014 during a Visegrad Scholarship at the Central European University in Budapest.

Notes

1 Outdated terms such as transsexualism or gender dysphoria were part of sexological vocabulary in the 1980s and were constitutive of the phenomena described

in this chapter. Therefore, I decided to use them when talking about sexological diagnoses.

When talking about the persons who were pursuing diagnoses, I use the word transgender, as an umbrella term for different types of gender nonconforming desires and behaviours.

2 *Zespół adwokacki* was an intermediary form between capitalist law firms and state-controlled attorneys in the USSR.

3 Reference to Julian Tuwim's 1933 poem.

4 Founder of the first gender clinic, inventor of the concept of gender, believed that gender identity is entirely the product of socialization. Controversial because of the tragic case of David Reimer.

Bibliography

Benjamin, Harry. 1966. *The Transsexual Phenomenon*. New York: Julian Press.

Dulko, Stanisław. 1982. "Stwierdzenie Zmiany Płci w Drodze Sądowej." *Nowe Prawo* 9 (10): 71–76.

Eckhert, Erik. 2016. "A Case for the Demedicalization of Queer Bodies." *The Yale Journal of Biology and Medicine* 89 (2): 239–46.

Epstein, Steven. 2003. "Sexualizing Governance and Medicalizing Identities: The Emergence of 'State-Centered' LGBT Health Politics in the United States." *Sexualities* 6 (2): 131–71.

Fidelis, Małgorzata. 2010. *Women, Communism, and Industrialization in Postwar Poland*. Cambridge: Cambridge University Press.

Funk, Nanette. 2014. "A Very Tangled Knot: Official State Socialist Women's Organizations, Women's Agency and Feminism in Eastern European State Socialism." *European Journal of Women's Studies* 21 (4): 344–360.

Ghodsee, Kristen. 2014. "Pressuring the Politburo: The Committee of the Bulgarian Women's Movement and State Socialist Feminism." *Slavic Review* 73 (3): 538–562.

Ghodsee, Kristen. 2019. *Second World, Second Sex: Socialist Women's Activism and Global Solidarity During the Cold War*. Durham, NC: Duke University Press.

Grabowska, Magdalena. 2012. "Bringing the Second World In: Conservative Revolution(s), Socialist Legacies, and Transnational Silences in the Trajectories of Polish Feminism." *Signs: Journal of Women in Culture and Society* 37 (2): 385–411.

Grabowska, Magdalena. 2018. *Zerwana genealogia. Działalność społeczna i polityczna kobiet po 1945 r. a współczesny ruch kobiecy*. Warszawa: Wydawnictwo Naukowe Scholar.

Haan, Francisca de. 2010. "Continuing Cold War Paradigms in Western Historiography of Transnational Women's Organisations: The Case of the Women's International Democratic Federation (WIDF)." *Women's History Review* 19 (4): 547–573.

Imieliński, Kazimierz. 1963. *Geneza homo- i biseksualizmu środowiskowego: teoria orientacji płciowej*. Warszawa: Państwowy Zakład Wydawnictw Lekarskich.

Imieliński, Kazimierz. 1980. *Seksuologia Kulturowa*. Warszawa: Państwowe Wydawnictwo Naukowe.

Imieliński, Kazimierz. 1985. *Seksuologia: Zarys Encyklopedyczny*. Warszawa: PWN.

Imieliński, Kazimierz. 1990. *Seksiatria*. Vol. 2. Warszawa: PWN.
Imieliński, Kazimierz, and Stanisław Dulko. 1988. *Przekleństwo Androgyne: transseksualizm—mity i rzeczywistość*. Warszawa: PWN.
Imieliński, Kazimierz, and Stanisław Dulko. 1989. *Apokalipsa płci*. Szczecin: Glob.
Imieliński, Kazimierz, Stanisław Dulko, and Wiesław Czernikiewicz. 1983. "Prawne Aspekty Małżeństwa Transseksualistów [Analiza Niezwykłego Przypadku]." *Nowe Prawo* 6: 69–71.
Kościańska, Agnieszka. 2014. *Płeć, przyjemność i przemoc: kształtowanie wiedzy eksperckiej o seksualności w Polsce*. Warszawa: Wyd. Uniwersytetu Warszawskiego.
Kulpa, Robert, and Joanna Mizielińska. 2016. *De-centring Western Sexualities: Central and Eastern European Perspectives*. London: Routledge.
Latour, Bruno. 1993. *We Have Never Been Modern*. Cambridge, MA: Harvard University Press.
Litwin, Jan. 1965. "Glosa Do Orzeczenia Sądu Wojewódzkiego Dla M.St Warszawy z 24 IX 1964." *Państwo i Prawo* 10: 602–610.
Meyerowitz, Joan. 1980. *How Sex Changed*. Cambridge, MA: Harvard University Press.
Mizielińska, Joanna. 2016. "Travelling Ideas, Travelling Times: On the Temporalities of LGBT and Queer Politics in Poland and the 'West.'" In *De-Centering Western Sexualities: Central and Eastern European Perspectives*, edited by Joanna Mizielińska and Robert Kulpa, 85–106. London: Routledge.
Polish Supreme Court. 1983. "Uchwała Sądu Najwyższego Izba Cywilna z Dnia 25 Lutego 1978." *Orzecznictwo Sądów Polskich i Komisji Arbitrażowyc* 10: 514–518.
Renkin, Hadley Z. 2009. "Homophobia and Queer Belonging in Hungary." *Focaal. European Journal of Anthropology* 53: 20–37.
Renkin, Hadley Z. 2016. "Biopolitical Mythologies: Róheim, Freud, (Homo)Phobia, and the Sexual Science of Eastern European Otherness." *Sexualities* 19 (1–2): 168–189.
Rubin, Gayle. 2011. *Deviations: A Gayle Rubin Reader*. Durham, NC: Duke University Press.
Sharpe, Andrew N. 2002. *Transgender Jurisprudence: Dysphoric Bodies of Law*. London: Cavendish.
Spurlin, William J. 2019. "Queer Theory and Biomedical Practice: The Biomedicalization of Sexuality/The Cultural Politics of Biomedicine." *Journal of Medical Humanities* 40 (1): 7–20.
Szulc, Łukasz. 2018. *Transnational Homosexuals in Communist Poland: Cross-Border Flows in Gay and Lesbian Magazines*. Cham: Palgrave Macmillan.
Trouillot, Michel-Rolph. 2002. "'The Otherwise Modern: Caribbean Lessons from the Savage Slot,' in Critically Modern: Alternatives, Alterities, Anthropologies." In *Critically Modern: Alternatives, Alterities, Anthropologies*, edited by Bruce M. Knauft, 220–237. Bloomington: Indiana University Press.
Załęski, Paweł Stefan. 2012. *Neoliberalizm i Społeczeństwo Obywatelskie. Monografie Fundacji Na Rzecz Nauki Polskiej*. Toruń: Wydawnictwo Naukowe Uniwersytetu Mikołaja Kopernika.

7 "Treatment is possible and effective?"

Polish sexologists and queers in correspondence in late state socialism

Agnieszka Kościańska

In 1970, JB from Wrocław wrote to a sexologist: "Homosexuality is the most horrible sexual perversion. I experienced it personally, and consider this my life's tragedy . . . Can homosexuality be cured? I am sure that the answer is 'no' . . . Why do I have a hard time finding women attractive?" (quoted in Lew-Starowicz 1970a, 14).[1] The sexologist, Zbigniew Lew-Starowicz, answered: "Treatment is possible and effective, but the attention of a specialist must be sought early on" (14). Between 1969 and 1990, Lew-Starowicz ran a sex advice column in *Itd* (*Etc*), a highly popular, progressive student weekly. By the mid-1980s, his approach towards homosexuality had changed fundamentally: "Treatment is neither necessary, nor possible," he wrote (1985, 23).

I seek to answer questions that arise from reading Lew-Starowicz's sex column: What happened between 1970 and 1985 that made Lew-Starowicz, along with many other Polish sex experts, change their views? What brought about this change? Did it result from the transnational flow of medical knowledge, which shifted from perceiving homosexuality as an illness to its gradual depathologization or, perhaps, from local developments such as contact with queer patients? Finally, I ask about gender: was the shift the same in relation to male and female homosexualities?

The following argument is based on my archival research on Polish expert knowledge of sexuality (from the 1950s to the present) covering major academic sexological publications, popular sex manuals, and magazines running sex-related columns. In these sources, I looked for letters written by Polish homosexuals and the answers that they received in return.[2] Further, I conducted in-depth interviews with sexologists active in the 1970s and 1980s to whom the letters were addressed and who are still alive. Finally, I discussed sexological publications from the era with LGBTQ persons who remember the 1970s and the 1980s, mostly with members of a senior support group run by a Polish LGBTQ organization.

On the theoretical level, following Michel Foucault (1978), I assume the pivotal role of expert knowledge in the construction of sexuality. Unlike Foucault, however, I look for agency in patients, correspondents, and doctors. I show that new expert ideas resulted from a dialogue, often unequal, between patients/correspondents and doctors, as doctors attempted to speak to patients' concerns (Terry 1999; Oosterhuis 2000).

Answering letters: Polish sexology and its patient-oriented approach

Although Polish sexology dates back to the late nineteenth century, it was in the 1970s and the 1980s that it truly flourished (Kościańska 2014, 2016). The political situation contributed to its development. Not only were the 1970s a decade of relative openness to the West when sexologists had access to Western scientific publications and travelled abroad for conferences. It was also a time in which the Communist Party gradually adopted a more relaxed attitude toward sexual issues, combining it with a pro-family and pronatalist approach (Ignaciuk 2016) and giving sexologists funds to develop clinics and training programs. The political situation became very tense at end of the 1970s and in the early 1980s when an economic crash led to constant shortages of consumer goods, including food. The Communist Party had little to offer citizens except for sexual explicitness, which had the additional advantage of counteracting the increasingly powerful Catholic Church (Kościańska 2017).

Mainstream Polish sexology under late socialism represented a unique approach. As I have argued elsewhere (Kościańska 2014, 2016), it was highly patient-oriented, multidisciplinary, and holistic. Polish sexologists in late socialism adhered to the official pro-family line but never developed a network of medical units to hospitalize "delinquents," as did their Czechoslovakian colleagues in that period (Lišková 2016). Moreover, unlike their USSR counterparts, Polish sexologists did not organize any obligatory re-education programs for homosexuals (Essig 1999, 28–29; Stella 2015, 47–49).

The majority of sexological activity in Poland was focused on education. Sexologists were closely affiliated with the Planned Parenthood Association (PPA) and many of them worked in the Association's clinics. They published extensively in the mass media and authored popular sex, or marital, manuals. It is estimated that one Polish sex manual, published in 1978, sold seven million copies in a country of 38 million (Kościańska 2016). Patients

76 *Agnieszka Kościańska*

often saw a sexologist after reading his or her book, while public lectures and book launches drew crowds. Sexologists regularly received countless letters from readers. Lew-Starowicz built his career around these letters. On many occasions, including in conversation with me, he explained that his views were based on international scientific literature and on his own experiences as a doctor and a sex columnist.[3] He considered patients and correspondents to be a crucial source of knowledge and inspiration (Lew-Starowicz 1985, 5).

As a result of their pro-patient orientation, sexologists were exceptionally humanistic as physicians and therapists. They were likely to amend their scientific outlook based on their patients' needs and concerns (Kościańska 2016). Unfortunately, their unique methods and their openness towards patients did not prevent heteronormativity and homophobia on their part.[4] Yet, for many Polish queers, sexologists were the only hope and the sole source of information. Doctors tried to navigate between their patients' desires, conservative socialist policies, Catholic sentiments, and censorship.[5] When the time came, they stood up for their patients by taking a political stance.

"There are many men like myself": letters from homosexual men

The first queer letters addressed to sexologists were published in the late 1950s by *Radar*, a youth magazine established after the Thaw in the Eastern Bloc. They were addressed to Mikołaj Kozakiewicz, who later became the president of the PPA. In one of these early letters, a sailor from a port city wrote:

> I'm very handsome and the ladies go crazy for me. What of it, when I can't even bear looking at them. I'm a sailor and I could have a thousand chances, but I never take advantage of it. I adore boys, what with my looks comes quite easy. Suffice it to go to the "meeting point' that exists in every city.
>
> (Kozakiewicz 1964, 107)

Quoting the letter in his 1964 book, Kozakiewicz commented:

> Homosexuality is an age-old issue. Firstly, let us get rid, once and for all, of those labels and designations that judge and morally condemn: "a sin against nature," "the sin of sodomy," "unnatural debauchery," etc.
>
> (108)

He went on to criticize certain stereotypes about homosexuality saying, for instance, that not all homosexual men were effeminate. He also discussed how his homosexual correspondents felt about themselves. Some of them were very unhappy and contemplated suicide but others expressed pride, comparing themselves to Plato, Leonardo da Vinci, or Oscar Wilde (he never mentioned any Polish names).

After such an introduction, readers might have expected that the sexologist would ascertain there was nothing wrong with homosexuality. However, Kozakiewicz argued that it did transgress the norm, after all: "Homosexuality is undoubtedly an inversion, a variation of the norm in which the object of sexual desire is switched" (110). He encouraged homosexuals to undertake treatment in order to be able to marry and have children, and thus to live a fulfilling life (112–113). Somewhat incongruently, he concluded his chapter on homosexuality by describing the lives of his correspondents who were in stable relationships based on friendship and erotic attraction to their same-sex partners. He wrote, "Looking at homosexuality from the point of view of secular ethics, from a rational point of view, we should demand from the sexual and erotic life of people who suffer this anomaly the same that we demand from heterosexual persons" (115), implying that certain kinds of homosexual relations (stable, based on friendship and sexual attraction) constitute the socially desirable model. He stressed that only this kind of homosexuality could be accepted. Clearly, he placed a stable, monogamous relation at the top what Gayle Rubin called sexual hierarchy (Rubin 1984).

In the late 1950s and throughout the 1960s, Kozakiewicz's mixed message stood out. It was hard to find anything else on homosexuality, save for highly specialized medical publications (e.g. Imieliński 1965). The prolonged, in-depth conversation between sexologists and queer readers would start a bit later, in 1969, when Lew-Starowicz was hired by *Itd* to run its sex column.

Lew-Starowicz (1970a) started writing about homosexuality by publishing excerpts from letters written by JB from Wrocław (quoted earlier) and four other, equally unhappy readers. The selection contrasts with Lew-Starowicz's 1973 characterization of the letters he received. During his first three years as a columnist, he received 1,560 letters: 4 per cent of them were from "deviants," usually homosexuals. "The majority of authors of these letters demands the 'rehabilitation' of homosexuality so it is treated as a normal way of satisfying sexual needs; some ask for information about the reasons, symptoms and outcomes of homosexuality and other perverse forms" (1973, 20). Why then did Lew-Starowicz choose these negative letters, and not those demanding rights?

Lew-Starowicz suggested in a recent interview I conducted that he did so partly because of his patients: those who came to him saw homosexuality as an illness, although he saw them as trapped in heteronormative society. But I would argue that by stressing the suffering of homosexual patients he was able to have his article approved by the censors, as homosexuals' emancipatory claims were at odds with socialist, pro-family morality. In socialist Poland, every publication had to be pre-approved for its adherence to socialist doctrine, and in this case, to socialist morality (Szulc 2018, 101). Lew-Starowicz was very good at tricking censors, who only intervened in his articles for *ltd* three times over 20 years (Lew-Starowicz 2013). The 1970 article is a perfect example of his strategy. Like Kozakiewicz, Lew-Starowicz was sending his readers a mixed message. After asserting that "[t]reatment is possible and effective" (Lew-Starowicz 1970a, 14), he was able to convey a more nuanced message about homosexuality in the rest of his piece.

He did so by referring to studies by Alfred Kinsey, by Evelin Hooker, and by Cleland Ford and Frank Beach (Bayer 1981) that were broadly discussed in the US during this period, and which contributed to removing homosexuality from the American Psychiatric Association's *Diagnostic and Statistical Manual of Mental Disorders* (DSM) in 1973. Lew-Starowicz invoked Kinsey, whose research was well known among Polish sexologists (Imieliński 1965), when he wrote, "Homosexuality is one of the most prevalent disorders to normal development and the orientation of sexual desire" (Lew-Starowicz 1970a, 14). He developed this argument by mentioning Ford and Beach: "Some researchers . . . evoke similar phenomena among certain species of animals." Finally, he brought up Hooker's efforts to show that on the psychological level there was no difference between homo- and heterosexuals: "shocked by the massive scale of this phenomenon, [some researchers] attempt to locate it in the field of psychosexual norms." Having presented these Western findings, Lew-Starowicz made certain to explicitly distance himself from them: "It is difficult to agree with these suggestions. In the sexual lives of animals this is a very marginal problem that occurs primarily in conditions of captivity, and then merely as a substitute." Nevertheless, he described the way homosexuality functioned in the West: "This phenomenon appears in many countries, and in some it has even gained the right to citizenship in the form of lenient criminal proceedings, special magazines and clubs designated for homosexuals, along with profiled cafes, beaches and various associations" (14). The passage is a typical example of playing games with censors. Like other authors, Lew-Starowicz attempted to communicate with readers without triggering a ban. Officially, everything Western was bourgeois and therefore at odds with socialist morality. But readers were eager to learn what was going on in the West, whose artefacts and lifestyle were desirable. Often, this curiosity was satisfied by presenting aspects of the West as outrageous. Such tactics are evident in the article: reinforced on all sides by assurances that homosexuality was a treatable condition, it yet announced the existence of gay bars and gay associations in the West. Bringing up this fact was a way of responding to the letters that could not be published, those that demanded acceptance for homosexuals. Lew-Starowicz was letting their authors and others know that the West was already offering what they wished for.

Five years later, in another article about homosexuality, Lew-Starowicz followed a similar format without citing any letters. He again presented homosexuality in a positive light but in a convoluted way. His approach was more affirmative and there was no mention of treatment. Rather, he focused on different attitudes toward homosexuality: positive in ancient Greece and negative ones in Prussia. For Poles in the 1970s it was clear that Prussia (and Germany in general) represented the enemy.[6] By contrast, ancient Greece was perceived as a place of art, high culture and general sophistication. Lew-Starowicz reiterated the link between homosexuality and artistic inclinations also locally: "In Poland, approaches towards homosexuality vary. In some circles, for example, among artists, there is evident tolerance. Other circles display indifference, but there are also some which demand severe punishment or compulsory medical treatment." Finally, he blamed society for the problems that his patients faced: "The lack of tolerance, understanding and respect towards otherness frequently leads to tragic ends (mental disorders, suicides)" (Lew-Starowicz 1975, 20).

The homosexual was therefore associated with the West, ancient Greece and the world of art, all of which had positive connotations in Poland of the 1970s. At the same time, society was presented as the source of homosexuals' suffering. Men from the senior LGBTQ support group remembered these articles. They told me that while they did not like being portrayed as ill, it was really important for them to learn about homosexuals who were artists and about other cultural contexts, especially in the West, and to read letters from other queers (see Basiuk in this volume). In contrast to other publications on homosexuality (Szulc 2018), Lew-Starowicz's articles treated homosexuality seriously, creating a space for first-hand queer voices to be heard. This approach encouraged homosexuals to send more letters demanding their rights. Once the Communist Party permitted sexual explicitness in the late 1970s, those letters appeared in print. Their authors no longer wanted to change; they wanted society to change instead.

A man named Igor wrote in 1978, "a glass of cognac, a young and handsome man, intoxicated with alcohol and companionship, an invitation for a night together. . . . Next, other encounters usually filled with pleasure" (quoted in Lew-Starowicz 1978, 30). He went on to describe his situation:

> From time to time, I succumb to meeting up with a man. It comes easy in the sort of arrangement I have. Escaping into another world fills me with happiness. These secretive meetings with various young men give me access to a range of sexual, social, cognitive and psychological experiences.
>
> (30)

However, Igor chose to marry a woman:

> Life without my family, wife, children and home would not make any sense as it would be empty without these things, which are also very beautiful. They bring me joy and warmth and enable me to be there for someone. To love and to give that which makes others happy.

Igor concluded his letter with a sort of manifesto:

> There are many men like myself, as I learned time and time again. Does a sexual dualism in which family life receives the greater weight deserve severe criticism? I know that it goes contrary to the general-societal norms, but is it not time to break with these canons and give approval to that which perhaps many people miss when they seek happiness? . . . Each of us has the right to what we deem beautiful. Why should societal norms restrict our experience? Is it not time for these barriers to break?
>
> (30)

Igor's letter was the earliest first-hand description of homosexual life combined with a rights claim on behalf of the male homosexual community to be published in mainstream Polish press.

In his reply published in *Itd*, Lew-Starowicz did not say anything about curing homosexuality. Instead, he expressed dissatisfaction with the selfish way Igor treated his wife. "In demanding changes to social norms he would surely expect to be accepted by his wife. What if she, too, had aims of her own, similar to his?" (30). That, Lew-Starowicz suggested, would be a threat to the family. Lew-Starowicz thus continued Kozakiewicz's position that sexuality should be realized within the bounds of a loving relationship or family. But he also thought society should refrain from being excessively harsh on homo- and bisexual men. "Societies in which the heterosexual and monogamous relationship is the accepted and expected model can be defensive towards otherness threatening that model. . . . This self-defence should not take on the characteristics of an inquisition; it must not be ruthless" (30). Although sceptical about Igor's lifestyle, Lew-Starowicz partly supported his manifesto.

In the following years, Lew-Starowicz changed his approach completely. In 1985, he wrote that he had received many letters asking about homosexuality. He divided them into three categories: letters from homosexuals who did not know what to do with their desires and felt alienated from society, letters from women who wanted handsome male homosexuals to become heterosexuals, and finally, letters from homosexuals who demanded rights and acceptance. He commented, "Homosexuality is neither an illness, nor a sexual deviation. . . . It is a psychosexual difference; an atypical form of sexual behaviour. . . . In the vast majority of cases, treatment is neither necessary nor possible" (Lew-Starowicz 1985, 23).

Although sexologists limited their acceptance and depathologization of homosexuality to stable, monogamous relationships, a major shift obviously took place in the sexological approach to homosexuality between the early 1970s and the mid-1980s. This may not seem surprising because the American Psychiatric Association had removed homosexuality from its DSM more than ten years previously. But Communist countries did not follow American regulations, while the World Health Organization continued to see homosexuality as an illness up till the early 1990s. Moreover, in the mid-1980s the Polish government launched a massive anti-homosexual campaign (dubbed "Hyacinth") using HIV/AIDS for an excuse (Szulc 2018; see also Morawska in this volume). In both North America and Western Europe, the backlash against LGBTQ rights was a fact in the 1980s (see, e.g., Weeks 1989, 301). But for Polish sexologists, influenced by their contacts with queer patients and correspondents, the 1980s was a period of progressive change.

"Does this mean I have lesbian tendencies?": emotional, secret, invisible

The statements and letters quoted earlier refer to homosexuality in general but they focus almost exclusively on men. Little was said specifically about lesbians before the early 1970s; when female homosexuality was discussed at all, it was presented separately from male homosexuality.

Lew-Starowicz first cited a lesbian voice in *Itd* in 1970, two months after his piece on (male) homosexuality. Like some of the men quoted earlier, an anonymous author wished to be cured:

> I'm a lesbian. I'm in despair. It's a terrible thing for a woman to feel physically attracted to another woman. I don't know what I need to do

in order to become a normal human being again. I'm in love with a woman, but she doesn't know about it. . . . I'm sexually driven to her. I can't imagine life without her. . . . How can I be cured? I want to be normal like other women.

(Lew-Starowicz 1970b, 14)

Lew-Starowicz approached lesbian experience in a completely different manner than male homosexuality (or homosexuality in general). Besides some references to ancient Greece, known from his articles on men, he defined the issue as follows:

> Lesbian love, as it is called, is female homosexuality. Its specific trait is intense secrecy. It has been around for a long time, with lineage reaching back to the famous Greek poetess Sappho from the island of Lesbos. It was known throughout the ages and has been a subject in the arts, for example in Courbet's beautiful nineteenth century painting. Yet it is shrouded in mystery. In contrast to male homosexuality, it does not reveal itself. Female patients rarely if ever visit the doctor's office to cure themselves of their perversion. This may be explained by women's greater secretiveness and the greater durability of lesbian relationships.

(14)

He also placed lesbianism in a romantic/emotional setting:

> Emotional dominance and mutual attachment form a strong bond that withstands the test of time. Here, the yearning for romantic feeling is realized.

(14)

Like in the case of homosexual men, Lew-Starowicz ended with stressing the abnormality of lesbianism:

> But the lesbian relationship is a deformation of the sexual drive and sexuality. It distorts the correct orientation of the sexual drive, which is directed towards the heterosexual relationship and procreation.

(14)

The message of the two 1970s articles was different: although both male and female homosexuality was perceived as an illness, in the case of men it was strongly and clearly defined (often by the lack of acceptance) and combined with the picture of bars, beaches, and associations in the West that might lead to the construction of an identity. In the case of women, some positive identity models also existed (Courbet's paintings, Sappho). But they were blurry, presented as Platonic, emotional (a sort of friendship), and secretive—so secretive that lesbians did not need sexological help (see Staroszczyk in this volume for more on lesbian unintelligibility). This approach to female homosexuality was developed in an article published in 1975, which cited a letter by a Warsaw-based woman named Mariola. "I'm a shy but attractive girl, they say. I am a university student. But I'm not happy and I feel lost. Living in a dorm was a nightmare for me," she confesses, as she had to witness her roommates having sex with boys. In effect, she moved into "a sublet room, with a girlfriend" (quoted in Lew-Starowicz 1976, 30). This is how Mariola described her desires:

> I always dreamed of a subtle, gentle and decent boy. Unfortunately, my relations end very quickly. The boys I meet and like only want sex. I don't even enjoy their caresses—they're too quick and too brutal, while I know that I am easily aroused and just fondling my breasts is enough for me to orgasm, which I've often reached by myself. A girlfriend of mine discovered my secret. She, too, is disappointed with boys and was never able to orgasm while having sex with them.
> (30)

They both decided to try sex without boys:

> We began sleeping in the same bed together because of the cold. She was the one who initiated the fondling. At first, we pretended that we were doing it in our dreams, but now turning off the lights is enough for us. Does this mean I have lesbian tendencies? . . . Maybe my friend is a lesbian? Please help me.
> (30)

Lew-Starowicz offered Mariola two options: "The first option is to continue your previous sexual life, which will most likely lead to the development of a homosexual orientation. The second, to cease this form of satisfying your sexual needs and to break up with your friend." He also opined, "the author of the letter developed a negative opinion of men much too quickly," suggesting that Mariola and her girlfriend should give boys a second chance: "both of them could reach sexual satisfaction through intercourse with their partners by means of foreplay" (30).

These two letters and the expert responses are the only direct addresses of female homosexuality in the 20 years of Lew-Starowicz's weekly column in *Itd*. Other instances, equally rare, are when female homosexuality is mentioned in the context of women's sexual frigidity (Lew-Starowicz 1983) and sexual life in a harem (Lew-Starowicz 1989), neither example offering an adequate picture of lesbianism.

Conclusions

During my conversations with LGBTQ seniors, they often recalled the sexological columns and books from the time of state socialism. They rarely appreciated the medical, pathologizing framework in which sexologists put homosexuality. However, they read sexologists' work and recall it today as important because it was their only source of information. They remembered being excited about mentions of homosexuality in sexological books. They liked reading about ancient Greece and gay clubs in the West. They appreciated the positive valuation implied in the staple homosexual being presented as perhaps ill but also a sensitive artist. You might try to cure yourself, but if that did not succeed, it was still possible to build a stable relation with a same-sex partner. This contrasted with how they were perceived by others: "as fags who wanted to have sex with children," as one senior gay man phrased it. A lesbian, who also remembered the 1970s, told me that when she understood that she liked girls more than boys she really wanted to learn as much as possible about homosexuality. She found some literary examples but her main source of concrete knowledge about sex was the column in *Itd* and one of the sexology books. Reading popular magazines was unproblematic but buying or borrowing books about sexuality from the library was too shameful. She would go to a bookshop, hide between the shelves and there read some excerpts so nobody would see her.

There is no doubt that sexological writings in the 1970s and 1980s were important to queer readers and contributed to homosexual liberation. The influence of sexology, however, had its limits. For many, it was too pathologizing. Genuine community and a real sense of gay and lesbian identity started with LGBTQ organizations that proliferated after 1989, although some foundational work occurred already in the late 1980s (Szulc 2018). When talking to senior gays and lesbians, I often heard, "I became really gay when Lambda started" or "the first Lambda meeting was a revelation."[7]

In the end, the sexological heritage of socialism is ambiguous. Although sexologists provided some positive models, they restricted homosexual liberation to stable, monogamous relationships and they almost entirely omitted women. However, faced with growing homophobia in recent years, sexologists, including Lew-Starowicz, who remains a major figure of Polish sexology, issued public statements supporting LGBTQ rights and published medical handbooks concerning homosexuality that fully encompass the equality of homosexual patients (Kowalczyk, Tritt, and Lew-Starowicz 2016).

Acknowledgements

Writing this chapter was possible thanks to a Royal Society Edinburgh/ Caledonian Research Fund European Visiting Research Fellowship at Edinburgh College of Art in Spring 2017. Many thanks to my colleagues from the CRUSEV research team, especially to Tomasz Basiuk, Glyn Davis, and Benny Nemerofsky Ramsay, for inspiring discussions about the letters analyzed in this chapter. An earlier version of this chapter was presented at the University of Glasgow in April 2017 and at the "How to Do the History of Sex" workshop at Edinburgh College of Art in May 2017. I am grateful to Marta Rozmysłowicz for translating the letters and polishing my English writing.

Notes

1 Excerpts from letters to sexologists and their answers were translated from Polish into English by Marta Rozmysłowicz.
2 Because I use terms common in the 1970s and the 1980s, I refrain from using the word "gay," as it hardly existed at the time in Polish. By contrast, the word "lesbian" was used widely by both sexologists and their correspondents.
3 As a member of the PPA, Lew-Starowicz was aware of developments in the West. Since its founding in 1957, the PPA was one of the most internationally connected institutions in socialist Poland (Kuźma-Markowska 2013). Focused primarily on family planning, it also dealt with other sexuality-related issues and employed a number of sexologists, including Lew-Starowicz, who consulted patients on all sorts of sexual problems, homosexuality included. Lew-Starowicz told me that, thanks to the planned parenthood networks, he had access not only to new research but to gay and lesbian liberation pamphlets.
4 And sexism, as I demonstrated elsewhere (2016).
5 Like other Eastern Bloc countries, socialist Poland introduced multiple progressive laws and policies: abortion and contraception were officially available, the legal change of sex was relatively easy, and gender reassignment surgery was covered by the state. Unlike the USSR, Poland did not criminalize homosexual acts. However, sexually explicit topics were banned from the public sphere; pornographic films and literature were illegal. The only acceptable form of sexuality was within marriage and linked to procreation.
6 During the entire period of state socialism, the Polish Communist Party engaged in strong anti-German propaganda. School children read patriotic prose and poetry from the nineteenth century, which was strongly anti-German/Prussian, and public TV (the only one available at the time) constantly showed World War II movies.
7 A major Polish gay and lesbian organization at the time.

Bibliography

Bayer, Ronald. 1981. *Homosexuality and American Psychiatry: The Politics of Diagnosis*. Princeton, NJ: Princeton University Press.

Essig, Laurie. 1999. *Queer in Russia*. Durham, NC: Duke University Press.

Foucault, Michel. 1978. *The History of Sexuality, Vol. 1: The Will to Knowledge*. Translated by R. Hurley. New York: Pantheon Books.

Ignaciuk, Agata. 2016. "Reproductive Policies and Women's Birth Control Practices in State-Socialist Poland (1960s–1980s)." In *"Wenn die Chemie stimmt." Gender Relations and Birth Control in the Age of the "Pill,"* edited by Lutz Niethammer and Silke Satjuko, 271–294. Göttingen: Wallstein.

Imieliński, Kazimierz. 1965. *Zboczenia płciowe (i ich korelacje z psychonerwicami): dynamiczna teoria zboczeń płciowych*. Warszawa: Państwowy Zakład Wydawnictw Lekarskich.

Kościańska, Agnieszka. 2014. "Beyond Viagra: Sex Therapy in Poland." *Sociologický časopis/Czech Sociological Review* 50 (6): 919–938.

Kościańska, Agnieszka. 2016. "Sex on Equal Terms? Polish Sexology on Women's Emancipation and 'Good Sex' from the 1970s to Present." *Sexualities* 19 (1–2): 236–256.

Kościańska, Agnieszka. 2017. *Zobaczyć łosia. Historia polskiej edukacji seksualnej od pierwszej lekcji do internetu*. Wołowiec: Czarne.

Kowalczyk, Robert, Remigiusz Jarosław Tritt, and Zbigniew Lew-Starowicz, eds. 2016. *LGB: zdrowie psychiczne i seksualne*. Warszawa: Wydawnictwo Lekarskie PZWL.

Kozakiewicz, Mikołaj. 1964. *Rozmowy intymne*. Warszawa: Państwowy Zakład Wydawnictw Lekarskich.

Kuźma-Markowska, Sylwia. 2013. "Międzynarodowe aspekty działalności Towarzystwa Świadomego Macierzyństwa w latach 50. i 60. XX w." In *Problem kontroli urodzeń i antykoncepcji. Krytyczno-porównawcza analiza dyskursów*, edited by Bożena Płonka-Syroka and Aleksandra Szlagowska. Wrocław: Uniwersytet Medyczny im. Piastów Śląskich we Wrocławiu.

Lew-Starowicz, Zbigniew. 1970a. "Homoseksualizm." *Itd* 8: 14.

Lew-Starowicz, Zbigniew. 1970b. "Miłość lesbijska." *Itd* 17: 14.

Lew-Starowicz, Zbigniew. 1973. "Listy do seksuologa (2)." *Itd* 10: 20.

Lew-Starowicz, Zbigniew. 1975. "Homoseksualizm." *Itd* 22: 20.

Lew-Starowicz, Zbigniew. 1976. "Miłość lesbijska." *Itd* 47: 30.

Lew-Starowicz, Zbigniew. 1978. "Inaczej." *Itd* 52–53: 30.

Lew-Starowicz, Zbigniew. 1983. "Ukryty homoseksualizm." *Itd* 23: 22–23.

Lew-Starowicz, Zbigniew. 1985. "Homoseksualizm." *Itd* 4: 22–23.

Lew-Starowicz, Zbigniew. 1987. "Homoseksualizm (lesbijstwo)." *Zwierciadło* 29: 12.

Lew-Starowicz, Zbigniew. 1989. "Homoseksualizm na Wschodzie." *Itd* 8: 23.

Lew-Starowicz, Zbigniew. 2013. *Pan od seksu*. Kraków: Znak.

Lišková, Kateřina. 2016. "'Now You See Them, Now You Don't.' Sexual Deviants and Sexological Expertise in Communist Czechoslovakia." *History of the Human Sciences* 29 (1): 49–74.

Oosterhuis, Harry. 2000. *Stepchildren of Nature: Krafft-Ebing, Psychiatry, and the Making of Sexual Identity*. Chicago: University of Chicago Press.

Rubin, Gayle. 1984. "Thinking Sex: Notes for a Radical Theory of the Politics." In *Pleasure and Danger: Exploring Female Sexuality*, edited by Carole S. Vance. London: Routledge & Kegan Paul.

Stella, Francesca. 2015. *Lesbian Loves in Soviet and Post-Soviet Russia*. London: Palgrave Macmillan.

Szulc, Łukasz. 2018. *Transnational Homosexuals in Communist Poland: Cross-Border Flows in Gay and Lesbian Magazines*. Cham: Palgrave Macmillan.

Terry, Jennifer. 1999. *An American Obsession: Science, Medicine, and Homosexuality in Modern Society*. Chicago: University of Chicago Press.

Weeks, Jeffrey. 1989. *Sex, Politics and Society: The Regulation of Sexuality since 1800*. 2nd ed. London: Longman.

8 "No authorities are interested in us, no one interferes in our affairs?"

Policing homosexual men in the People's Republic of Poland

Karolina Morawska

Introduction

"I am a young Polish man.... While your magazine ... has not been arriving regularly, I have remained a faithful reader for the past few years.... In a number of big Polish cities homosexuals are a completely normal phenomenon which does not upset the public. But you should know that it is the general backwardness of public opinion rather than any legal regulation that is keeping us from being more visible," reads a 1962 letter sent by Czesław, a student from Cracow, to the editor of *Der Weg zu Freundschaft und Toleranz* (*Road to Friendship and Tolerance*). He goes on, "There are plenty of us here, homosexuals. No authority, whether at state level or the militia [i.e. socialist state police], is interested in us or interferes in our affairs." (Institute for National Remembrance, File Access Bureau [hereinafter "IPN BU"] 0236/142/4, quoted in Tomasik 2018, 15).

Czesław's account suggests that the circumstances of homosexual persons in the People's Republic of Poland were favourable when compared with other Eastern Bloc countries: he emphasizes the lack of any repressions by the police or state authorities. The optimistic tone of the letter may have something to do with Czesław's young age (32 years) and the fact that he lived in a big city, where meeting new people was not difficult, and where he might not have fallen victim to intolerance. Yet documents preserved at the Institute for National Remembrance, created by officials at the Ministry of Internal Affairs and members of its police force (MO)[1] reveal an entirely different picture of homosexuals' daily life.

Today, the state-socialist authorities' interest in the gay community is associated chiefly with the surveillance of political opponents by the Security Service of the Ministry of Internal Affairs and with the notorious mass operation codenamed "Hiacynt" (Hyacinth) on 16 and 17 November 1985, repeated the next and the following year (26 and 27 September 1986, and 16 and 17 November 1987; see Szulc 2018, 107; Majewska 2018, 55–56). Operation Hyacinth is now regarded as the most spectacular symptom and the central symbol of homosexual men's persecution by state-socialist police. An analysis of police and Ministry of Internal Affairs documents from the 1960s, 1970s, and 1980s indicates that Hyacinth was an apex of repression and surveillance work which the police had engaged in for decades. My key objective is to understand this process by analysing the officials' discourse. Notably, the repressive measures used had been planned at the top, as I demonstrate. Rather than ordinary cases of violence rooted in bias or conservative outlook, my source analysis points to an organized system of controlling the male homosexual community. In the eyes of Communist authorities, excessive visibility and self-organization efforts of homosexual men would have breached the nation's moral and political unity. (Homosexual women were rarely targeted for reasons I clarify shortly.) Scholars addressing Operation Hyacinth usually focus on the sequence of events and its effects, including its subversive importance for the origins of the LGBT movement in Poland (Mrok 1999; Kurpios 2003, 4; Tomasik 2018, 42–51; Selerowicz 2015; Kościańska 2017, 229–239). However, our knowledge of preparations and reasons for the campaign remains incomplete. In seeking to address these questions, I focus on never-before analysed documents of the state police in order to reconstruct its discourse on homosexuality. Of all police files preserved at the Institute for National Remembrance, the oldest homosexuality-related papers date back to the years 1962–1963. In all likelihood, the Ministry of Internal Affairs began to organize its knowledge about the "homosexuality phenomenon" at the time (see Tomasik 2018, 57) and that is when I begin my investigation. I stop with the Operation Hyacinth in 1985.

In what follows, I briefly sketch the social and moral backdrop of the time. Changing attitudes to homosexuality in the People's Republic of Poland have been addressed by others (Szulc 2018, 93–117; Kościańska 2017; Tomasik 2018). However, the state police perspective, a focal point for my deliberations, has scarcely been explored. I fill this gap by examining documents created by the Ministry of Internal Affairs and state police representatives for information and training purposes. I trace the developing knowledge of the "homosexuality phenomenon" (an official label), its theoretical assumptions, expert recommendations, the sources of information used, and—last but not least—ways that these official recommendations were put into practice and affected the daily life of homosexuals. I analyse the discursive construction of the homosexual, especially the alleged criminogenic nature of the so-called homosexual milieu.[2] My analysis of documents accessed at the Institute for National Remembrance is supplemented by oral history testimonies from homosexual men discussing the forms of repression actually applied by police officers. Of course, my sources in no way warrant statistically meaningful conclusions concerning the extent to which the gay community was exposed to surveillance. Nonetheless, they offer a crucial glance into police activity prior to the infamous Operation Hyacinth, including theoretical assumptions and specific instructions, as well as concrete repressive practices and their effects on queer individuals.

The backdrop

Nonconformity—sexual difference included—had no place in "healthy" socialist society, and so homosexuality was taboo in the People's Republic of Poland, lacking official recognition (Więch 2005, 257–264; see Morawska 2019). The lack of recognition was rooted in the absence of penalization. At the same time, the morally conservative Communist authorities regarded any divergence from generally accepted norms to be a breach of the social and political order, even if no law was broken. In practice, the official line was to pretend homosexuality did not exist while investigating it, partly to recruit assets and blackmail political opponents (Fiedotow 2012, 241). Thus, despite the absence of official policy, the actions taken by the authorities were far from random.

There was a fundamental difference in the approach to homosexuality by Party authorities and the Security Service on the one hand, and by state police officers on the other. The former saw homosexuals as easy to blackmail and as potential collaborators. Knowledge of one's sexual life, typically of the elite, was a tool of political manipulation. By contrast, the activity of the police was grounded in the view of the homosexual milieu as intrinsically criminogenic (as described e.g. by criminologist JS Giza 1963; see Fiedotow 2012, 271). This view justified that it should be closely monitored. As noted by Agata Fiedotow, these different motivations for policing homosexuality occasionally overlapped but were considered separate matters (2012, 271).

Surveillance instructions

Operation Hyacinth, a mass campaign in which numerous queer men were forcibly brought to police stations across the country, questioned, and formally registered as homosexuals, all within a day or two, was first staged by the police in 1985. The effort was among the very last attempts to create a register of homosexual persons and, by the same token, it brought into relief the officials' helplessness before the phenomenon they were tackling. Scholars disagree about when the police first took an interest in the homosexual community. Paweł Kurpios argues that the community fell under surveillance in the 1970s, whereas according to Agata Fiedotow, the first attempts date back to the previous decade (Kurpios 2003, 3; Fiedotow 2012, 271). Having analyzed documents preserved at the Institute for National Remembrance, I am inclined to side with Agata Fiedotow; yet one should bear in mind the likelihood that sources have been overlooked. Keyword searches in the Institute for National Remembrance archive yield limited results and valuable files are discovered by chance. Moreover, the whereabouts of some sources, including the documents created during Operation Hyacinth, remains unknown (Majewska 2018, 57).

The earliest known papers documenting the Ministry's of Internal Affairs interest in homosexuality date back to the years 1962–1963: they are kept at the Institute for National Remembrance in several files marked "Homosexual Milieu." However, among these papers are lists naming mostly male homosexuals known to the police that were compiled in the previous decade (Tomasik 2018, 55–56; see Ryziński 2018).

Information gathered on the "homosexuality phenomenon" in Poland was first given synthetic form in November 1963, in a training script issued by the Department of Human Resources and Training of the Ministry of Internal Affairs, co-authored by Colonel Adam Krukowski, MA, Professor Bolesław Popielski, PhD., Major Artur Solarz, MA, and Colonel Ryszard Zelwiański, PhD. It was titled *Homoseksualizm* (*Homosexuality* 1963). The brochure was based on writings on homosexuality by Polish and foreign criminologists (Witschi 1961; Kosyra 1962; Exner 1949; Giza 1963) and on reports and evidence gathered by the Criminal Service Department at central police headquarters.

In the foreword, the authors acknowledge that the Ministry's understanding of homosexuality is limited given the subject's complexity and the fact that it had mostly been ignored before. They seek to explain it with pathologizing medical language, as when they define homosexuality as "sexual deviation" and delve into its alleged biological causes. They also suggest a glossary of synonyms for "homosexuality" and "homosexual," such as "pederasts," "urnings," "homoeroticism," "sexual inversion," "lesbian love," and "sapphism" (7).

The brochure is one of the few wherein authors reference homosexual women, albeit they pay them little attention, justifying this limited interest with mentions of female "caution and temperance," "propensity for monogamous love" (which is why lesbians "do not form organised communities"), and asserting that women "are free of the typically male and exceedingly strong moment of aggression"; finally, "the social scourge of lesbian vagrants is more rare" than the more troubling male homosexual drifters (46, 11). As explained in the brochure, this itinerant community primarily includes runaways from home and escapees from correctional and penitentiary institutions.

Crucially, the authors argue for the need to subject homosexual men to surveillance by pointing to the growing sex-crime rate, including same-sex crimes. As in other such brochures I have seen, the authors point to two issues which they consider inseparable—on the one hand, a homosexual may commit sex crimes, on the other, he may fall victim to a sex crime himself. The brochure lists same-sex crimes committed in the "homosexual milieu" with top examples being "eroticism-related manslaughter committed by homosexuals," "manslaughter of homosexuals by their partners" (with the annotation "much more frequent"), and "lewd acts involving minors" (56). Why do authors believe partners of homosexual men to be a threat?

> A variety of reasons, usually when jealousy comes into play, may cause serious or less serious conflicts, occasionally leading to criminal activity . . . (26–27). Some higher-class homosexuals seek commitment from their partners by describing or displaying their wealth, or with pecuniary promises; such behaviour may become a trigger of evil instincts in their partners, who are thus provoked to robbery, frequently tying in with murder.
>
> (50)

Authors of the brochure thus point to two fundamental motives that may lead to crime: jealousy or greed.

The authors see same-sex prostitution as a "breeding ground of assorted crime" (46), as the scene typically includes "vagrants, escapees from penitentiary institutions, petty criminals, etc.; 80% are heterosexual individuals using such contacts only as a source of income" (47). Linking the two phenomena—homosexuality and same-sex prostitution—is typical for state police discourse.

Last but not least, authors of the brochure concern themselves with young men "submitting to depravation by pure chance, then becoming homosexual" as a result of encountering "perverted individuals" (19). They recommend harsh penalties for lewd acts involving minors so as to prevent "the expansion of a new army of juvenile homosexuals developing acquired deviation of the sexual drive" (68). The authors find that men who choose professions "matching their deprived inclinations" are particularly dangerous: "homosexuals grouping within a single profession may influence individuals originally normal, especially if young—this is how the numbers of those who acquire homosexuality grows." Some male professions are named as especially dangerous: barbers, nurses, public bath and shower room attendants, teachers, soldiers, theatrical and film actors, ballet dancers and any "sizeable ensembles of young men with numerous occasions to be in the nude"; among female professions the nurses, homeroom mistresses, and teachers merit a special warning (19). But these are hardly the only risks threatening young people, as certain communities are infested with "something akin to more or less organised 'mafias'," their representatives setting the tone for the entire community and influencing "individuals originally displaying no homosexual tendencies"; even worse, such "precarious connections" have been shown to exist "between homosexuals from different communities, towns, or even countries . . . [sharing] a sense of solidarity and belonging to a flock of similar individuals" (26–27). Police officers thus display palpable fear of homosexual men's self-organizing, a theme I shall revisit.

In chapters describing ways of penalizing sexuality-related felonies and sex crimes (pimping, pandering, pornography, lewd acts involving minors, blackmail, abuse of dependency relations), warnings are issued against homosexual men "constantly on the prowl for new partners." Unlike those in stable relationships, the promiscuous are considered most dangerous and most numerous. While authors of the brochure are visibly averse to promiscuity, this does not prevent them from seeing men "constantly on the prowl for new partners" as potential victims, which in turn provides a pretext for keeping a close eye on this population:

> Big cities are conducive to such "cruising." A homosexual frequently changing partners is a target "particularly endangered" by his former partner as well as the current one encountered by chance. Such homosexuals fall victim to assorted forms of assault and coercion. They should remain under permanent police surveillance.
> (53)

The theme of crimes committed against homosexual men by strangers they invited into their homes surfaces in oral history testimonies. One interviewee, a resident of Warsaw in the 1970s, recalls:

> Such stuff is well-known, people even write about it, I heard of such cases, there was this guy—I don't know, some guy called Krzysiek? I never met him, but he met up with a guy at the Central Station, took him home and the guy murdered him to rob him, set fire to his body right there on the mattress, or something. I heard about his case, about this guy, but there were many more such cases.

Such situations offered a pretext for closer surveillance of the male homosexual community. Authors of the brochure express this view, albeit with something akin to distaste: "while this sounds illogical, it seems that the greater the civilization, the greater the number of homosexuals therein"— the sentence is underlined in the brochure (19). This observation is not a call for tolerance, however. It is followed by the stipulation that the ratio stems from grater prevalence of "acquired homosexuality" (19).

The chapter describing the Polish situation is especially interesting. While misbegotten attempts to tally gays in the bigger Polish cities may be amusing, the compilation of contemporaneous cruising sites is hugely valuable; many of these sites no longer exist, and yet they were enormously important in the lives of many homosexual men of the time. The brochure lists these locations (cafes, clubs, parks) in Cracow: *Pod Baranami, Kolorowa, Planty* Park; Warsaw: *Alhambra, Antyczna, Ali Baba, Ewa, Lajkonik, Roxana, Wilanowska*; Wrocław: *Szczytnicki* Park, central station neighbourhood, *Polonia*; Łódź: *Łodzianka, Akademicka, Kopciuszek*; and Katowice: *Agawa, Polonia, Cyganeria, Śnieżka* (39; see Tomasik 2018, 60–61). The listing instructed police officers to survey these spaces and recruit informants there.

In 1974 the Ministry of Internal Affairs issued *Prostytucja, homoseksualizm* (*Prostitution, Homosexuality*), the proceedings of a staff training conference in Szklarska Poręba. As usual, the themes of homosexuality and same-sex prostitution were linked. The authors, Zbigniew Niedaszkowski from police headquarters in Warsaw and Andrzej Rak from regional headquarters in Wrocław, quote the 1963 brochure word for word when relating information about homosexual persons. Their medical and pathologizing discourse is also the same, including the definition of homosexuality as "deviation of the sexual drive" (25). Polish and Austrian criminologists (e.g. Exner 1949; Giza 1963; Witschi 1961) and sexologists (Imieliński 1963) are referenced. Justifications of the supposed need to investigate the community are very similar as well. While the authors are aware that homosexuality is not punishable by law, they list the stipulations of the 1969 Criminal Code which they deem "potentially fully applicable in restricting the outreach of the negative phenomenon" (37). These provisions include the proscription of a lewd act involving a minor (Article 176), causing outrage with a lewd act (Article 177), pimping and pandering (Article 174), pornography (Article 173), forcible sexual behaviour (Article 167), rape (Article 168), a lewd act involving a certifiably insane person (Article 169), a lewd act involving abuse of a dependency relation (Article 170), exposure to a venereal disease (Article 162), and inducing drunkenness in a minor (Article 185). Clearly, these provisions were used against homosexual men, both for reasons rooted in homophobia and a propensity for bullying, and to gather information about the community by recruiting informants. Notably, the writers express their concern that the gay community's self-organizing has become more apparent:

> Commonly known meeting and cruising locations, etc. have been established... natural leaders have emerged, meetings are being organised [including] so-called Japanese evenings and sexual orgies... attempts are made to hold local and even national assemblies.
>
> (38)

Given police officers' propensity to exaggerate and their inclination to paint a picture of dangerous homosexuals, we cannot unreservedly trust their word. If what they report were true, the Polish gay community's attempts at self-organizing in the early 1970s would have long predated first official organizations. But the status of the "assemblies" is unclear and it may be that the police were misnaming primarily social gatherings as political. The remark nonetheless reveals that the police feared homosexuals organizing for political goals, rather than just to seek social and sexual contact. This concern, perhaps inflated, could well become a pretext for intimidation, expressed in regular surveillance and its apex, the Operation Hyacinth.

We learn that the regional police headquarters in Wrocław appointed the author Andrzej Rak of the Sixth Criminal Division to investigate homosexuals. Rak details his system of compiling a register of homosexual men, which apparently included working with owners of illegal liquor shops and "individuals profiting from prostitution." Such cooperation was described as "yielding top-notch results in terms of quality and quantity alike" (55). Rak contends that an officer's duty is limited to the monitoring of illegal liquor shops, railway and bus stations, and other "locations frequented by suspicious characters," organizing lookouts at locations "particularly threatened by activities of homosexuals and their satellites," "co-operating with other operational units to gather information," and, first and foremost, "keeping records of homosexual communities, homosexual prostitution included" (43–44). Categorizing a given individual as a same-sex prostitute is described as simple: the category should include persons engaging in sexual contact for monetary gain as well as anyone "remaining in a regular relationship with a homosexual person in exchange for lodging, food, clothing, and spending money . . . [adding that] homosexuals refer to such relationships as 'marriages,' [which] may last as long as several years" (55). In a reflection of their bias, the police clearly could not imagine homosexual persons forming permanent relationships ("marriages").

Officers saw all such relationships as pathological, and perhaps as motivated by material gain. Finally, the necessity of engaging in regular undercover work is emphasized as fundamental for properly investigating the homosexual community: "one-off missions are ineffectual," as "this milieu is hugely mobile, thriving, and covert" (55).

Evidence from oral history

The regular patrolling of cruising sites by state police officers, public lavatories in particular, is also a recurrent theme in oral history interviews. One interviewee, a resident of Poznań in the 1970s, recalls:

> I was once provoked by a plainclothes officer—he was in the restroom and pretended to be interested in me, and then he arrested [i.e. apprehended] me—he took me to the police station and wrote me up. I was a university student then, so the whole situation scared me a bit, but there were no [further] consequences. He was young, not in uniform, after all, in plain clothes. He took me to the police station to write me up, but no comments were made.

Another interviewee, a resident of Katowice and Cracow at the time, describes multiple summons to the police station in the early 1980s:

> The police knew everything about us, I was summoned to the precinct several times, not as part of the famous Hyacinth, but I was summoned a few times . . . my situation was easy, because my family knew . . . they [police officers] knew everything, but if you didn't provoke them you weren't summoned . . . they tried to intimidate me, they said they would tell my parents, so I said, "my parents know everything," then they said, OK, so we'll tell on you at work, so I said, I'll quit my job and find another one.

Notably, "provocation" did not necessarily mean engaging in any kind of suspicious activity: it would suffice for police officers to find one's address in the notebook of a man who had been apprehended or fallen victim to a crime.

When a homosexual man was murdered in Gdańsk, several hundred letters were found in his flat, all responding to an ad he placed in *Relaks i Kolekcjoner Polski*, a magazine publishing same-sex personal ads from 1983 onwards. All authors of letters found in the flat were immediately summoned for questioning; their personal data was recorded, they were photographed and fingerprinted (Eastern Europe Information Pool 1985, 9; Szulc 2018, 109; Morawska 2019). The character of the encounter with the police, including the level of intimidation, depended on the given officer. This is how such "hunts" are recalled by a homosexual man employed by the police in the years 1975–1978:

> What happened was that plainclothes officers would show up at a cruising site, they would pick up guys, and would then blackmail and recruit them. . . . If they got a person from a large company, especially someone with access to human resources files, well, he could prove valuable. So, you would try to recruit him. . . . And if the guy tried to give us the slip, we would say, listen here, I can take a little trip to your company, and drop this fucking piece of paper with your declaration on it, kind of by chance, and someone in your office could pick it up, you catching my drift?

Patrolling the homosexual community and keeping lists was not exclusive to the Polish state police. Special-purpose lists of homosexual persons were also compiled in Hungary, Czechoslovakia, the German Democratic Republic, and the Soviet Union (Szulc 2018, 75). In her article on the Czech LGBT community, Kateřina Nedbálková relates an account from a man blackmailed by the police:

> A guy called me out of the pub where I was having a beer with my friends. We were loud, I know, and we talked about all kinds of things. Outside he punched me in the head, said he was a policeman and that he was going to tell my parents and at my job that I am gay. I said he can do whatever he wants and then he left.
> (Nedbálková 2007, 67–80)

Mass registration campaigns of homosexuals such as Operation Hyacinth were not exclusive to the Polish state police, either. They were implemented when regular patrolling of cruising sites and one-off missions were deemed insufficient. Mass actions were organized in the German Democratic Republic in the 1980s in response to the newly born local gay movement. They were coded Operation Brother and Operation After Shave (Szulc 2018, 75; McLellan 2011, 134; Sweet 1995, 356; Stapel 1999). As described by Josie McLellan, homosexual relations as such were not necessarily the ultimate target; the police were rather after potential political activities among the community ("In short, they were worried about the possibility that gay rights groups would destabilise the regime"; McLellan 2011, 132).

Conclusions

While not all sources may be accessible and some may have been lost, the materials presented herein show that state police efforts to register all homosexual men were thriving and a coherent ideological basis for them had been formulated long before Operation Hyacinth. My evidence suggests that top-down, carefully planned, and consistently executed activities were intended to gather as much information on the homosexual community as possible and to recruit informants. Gradually, they morphed into massive operations intimidating the community, possibly inspired by similar campaigns organized in the German Democratic Republic and very likely motivated by fears—evidenced in police training scripts—that the community's political self-organization was afoot. This explanation was offered by Waldemar Zboralski, one of the first Polish LGBT activists: "I am absolutely convinced that the Operation [Hyacinth] was simply a response from those in power to independent gay initiatives in Poland and neighbouring countries aimed at forming official, openly gay groups" (Tomasik 2018, 51).

State-socialist police approach to homosexuality was dual in nature: the supposed necessity to monitor the community on a regular basis was justified by crimes committed by homosexual men on the one hand and by the need to protect them against criminals (such as robbers and murderers) on the other. The motif of constant threat was disseminated to such extent that it was finally used as justification for Operation Hyacinth. In a press article published on 12 January 1986 in the journal *W Służbie Narodu*, police headquarters spokesman Sławoj Kopka explained the decision to organize the campaign with the threat of venereal diseases and poor detection rate of perpetrators in homosexual homicide cases (the data he quoted suggested that the rate was approximately 50 per cent, as compared to 90 per cent for other homicides). He also issued a warning against a particularly dangerous character:

> The homosexuality phenomenon notwithstanding, a new and very dangerous character has reared his head; the thug [*żul*]. A thug is a young man whose main characteristic is his wish for an easy life. . . . He provides sexual services. He will often take advantage of a homosexual person's affability and blackmail him for the sake of financial gain. He may occasionally put the homosexual up as a mark for other thugs, who will then burglarise, rob, or even kill their victim.
>
> (Kopka 1986)

The events and far-ranging consequences of Operation Hyacinth do not fall within my purview here, as this chapter presents somewhat neglected and even some forgotten sources which show that the infamous campaign was a spectacular, as well as dramatic, climax of oppression engaged in by police officers over many years. However, it goes without saying that Operation Hyacinth yielded subversive results, unforeseeable to its organizers, sparking a modern LGBT movement in Poland. The activist Andrzej Selerowicz notes that its massive character helped destroy the illusion that staying in the closet could guarantee personal safety:

> Before Hyacinth, some people thought they were marvellously concealed. And then it turned out that if the state police decided they would unveil someone's double act, they would do it any time, any place. You can never remain fully hidden. This just went to show that it makes no sense to live in such hypocrisy and hiding.
>
> (Tomasik 2018, 50)

The terrifying witch-hunt, with its probable primary purpose of intimidating the community (as claimed by Zboralski; see Kościańska 2017, 230–237), brought results directly contrasting with its intent: early calls for liberation and appeals for tolerance rose directly in its wake and homosexual men began to fight for the right to self-organize. In the mid-1980s homosexuality would finally become a publicly debated issue.

Notes

1 The word "police" is used here for the sake of clarity even though in the People's Republic of Poland the regular police, established for purposes of fighting crime and securing public safety, was called Citizens' Militia (*Milicja Obywatelska*, abbreviated "MO"). The name was in use between 1944 and 1990.
2 The word "milieu" (*środowisko*) was consistently used by the Citizens' Militia, Security Service, and the Ministry of Internal Affairs. Its provenance is unclear but the term *Homosexuellenmilieu* was also used by Austrian criminologists, such as Hans Witschi (1961).

Bibliography

Dobrowolska, Anna. 2018. "Od 'Paragrafu zero' do 'Wolnego Zawodu.' Prostytucja i praca seksualna w PRL, 1956–1989." M.A. diss., University of Warsaw.
Exner, Franz. 1949. *Kriminologie*. Berlin, Göttingen, and Heindelberg: Hanseatische Verlagsanstalt.
Fiedotow Agata. 2012. "Początki ruchu gejowskiego w Polsce przełomu lat osiemdziesiątych i dziewięćdziesiątych XX wieku." In *Kłopoty z seksem w PRL. Rodzenie nie całkiem po ludzku, aborcja, choroby, odmienności*, edited by Marcin Kula, 241–358. Warszawa: Wyd. Uniwersytetu Warszawskiego.
Giza, Jerzy. 1963. "Prostytucja homoseksualna w świetle badań terenowych." *Państwo i Prawo* 18: 889–897.

Giza, Jerzy, and Wiesław Morasiewicz. 1968. "Homoseksualizm w środowisku więźniów młodocianych." *Przegląd penitencjarny* 4: 45–60.

Górniak, Krzysztof. 1982. "Wiktymologiczny aspekt zjawiska homoseksualizmu." M.A. diss., Warszawa: Instytut Kryminalistyki i Kryminologii ASW. IPN BU 001834/1654.

Homoseksualizm. Skrypt. 1963. Warszawa: Departament Kadr i Szkolenia MSW. IPN BU 01335/129.

ILGA's Eastern Europe Information Pool Report. 1985. www.transnationalhomosexuals.pl/reports.

Imieliński, Kazimierz. 1963. *Geneza homo i biseksualizmu środowiskowego. Teoria orientacji płciowej*. Warszawa: Państwowy Zakład Wydawnictw Literackich.

Jörgens, Frédéric. 2007. "*East* Berlin: Lesbian and Gay Narratives on Everyday Life, Social Acceptance, and Past and Present." In *Beyond the Pink Curtain. Everyday Life of LGBT People in Eastern Europe*, edited by Judit Takács and Roman Kuhar, 117–139. Ljubljana: The Peace Institute.

Kończyk, Sylwester. 1979. "Zabójstwo homoseksualisty w Szczecinie." In *Zabójstwa w Zbydniowie i Szczecinie*, 29–57. Warszawa: Departament Szkolenia i Doskonalenia Zawodowego MSW.

Kopka, Sławoj. 1986. "Hiacynt." *W Służbie Narodu* 2: 11–13.

Kościańska, Agnieszka. 2017. *Zobaczyć łosia. Historia polskiej edukacji seksualnej od pierwszej lekcji do internetu*. Wołowiec: Czarne.

Kosyra, Herbert. 1962. "Die Homosexualität—ein immer aktuelles Problem." *Kriminalistik* 2: 113.

Kurpios, Paweł. 2003. "Poszukiwani, poszukiwane. Geje i lesbijki a rzeczywistość PRL." *Zeszyty kulturoznawcze* 1: 27–34.

Majewska, Ewa. 2018. "Public Against Our Will? The Caring Gaze of Leviathan, 'Pink Files' from the 1980s Poland and the Issue of Privacy." *InterAlia* 13: 54–77.

Makowski, Wacław, ed. 1933. *Kodeks karny*. Warszawa: Drukarnia "Monolit".

McLellan, Josie. 2011. *Love in the Time of Communism: Intimacy and Sexuality in the GDR*. Cambridge: Cambridge University Press.

Milcke, Mikołaj. 2015. *Różowe kartoteki*. Słupsk: Wydawnictwo Dobra Literatura.

Morawska, Karolina. 2019. "*Którego serdeczna, uczciwa przyjaźń będzie motorem mojego życia* . . .—anonse towarzyskie w „Relaksie" z lat 1984–1988." *InterAlia* 14: 51–72.

Mrok, Marek. 1999. *Ruch gejowski w Polsce do 1989 (PRL) oraz ruch gejowski w III Rzeczpospolitej po 1989 do 1999*. Gdańsk: G-eye Team.

Nedbálková, Kateřina. 2007. "The Changing Space of the Gay and Lesbian Community in the Czech Republic." In *Beyond the Pink Curtain: Everyday Life of LGBT People in Eastern Europe*, edited by Judit Takács, Roman Kuhar, 67–80. Ljubljana: The Peace Institute.

Płatek, Monika. 2009. "Sytuacja osób homoseksualnych w prawie karnym." In *Orientacja seksualna i tożsamość płciowa*, edited by Roman Wieruszewski and Mirosław Wyrzykowski, 49–81. Warszawa: Instytut Wydawniczy EuroPrawo.

Prostytucja, homoseksualizm. Materiały kursokonferencji w Szklarskiej Porębie. 1974. Warszawa: Departament Szkolenia i Doskonalenia Zawodowego MSW. IPN BU 01522/305.

Report of the Eastern Europe Information Pool. Vienna 1982. https://docs.wixstatic. com/ugd/90d4c0_2b1299dc69874002bc7690877e9d08df.pdf.
Ryziński, Remigiusz. 2017. *Foucault w Warszawie. Dowody na Istnienie*.
Ryziński, Remigiusz. 2018. *Dziwniejsza historia*. Wołowiec: Czarne.
Selerowicz, Andrzej. 2015. *Kryptonim 'Hiacynt.'* Kraków: Wydawnictwo Queermedia.pl.
Stapel, Eduard. 1999. *Warme Brüder gegen Kalte Krieger: Schwulenbewegung in der DDR im Visier der Staatssicherheit*. Magdeburg: Landesbeauftragte für die Unterlagen des Staatssicherheitsdienstes der ehemaligen DDR Sachsen-Anhalt.
Sweet, Denis. 1995. "The Church, the Stasi and Socialist Integration: Three Stages of Lesbian and Gay Emancipation in the Former German Democratic Republic." In *Gay Men and the Sexual History of the Political Left*, edited by Gert Hekma, Harry Oosterhuis, and James Steakley, 351–367. New York: The Haworth Press.
Szulc, Łukasz. 2018. *Transnational Homosexuals in Communist Poland: Cross-Border Flows in Gay and Lesbian Magazines*. Cham: Palgrave Macmillan.
Tomasik, Krzysztof. 2018. *Gejerel*. Warszawa: Wydawnictwo Krytyki Politycznej.
Warkocki, Błażej. 2014. "Trzy fale emancypacji homoseksualnej w Polsce." *Porównania* 15: 121–132.
Więch, Arkadiusz. 2005. "Różowy odcień PRL-u. Zarys badań nad mniejszościami seksualnymi w Polsce Ludowej." In *Homoseksualizm—perspektywa interdyscyplinarna*, edited by Krystyna Slany, Beata Kowalska, and Marcin Śmietana, 257–264. Kraków: Nomos.
Witschi, Hans. 1961. "Das Homosexuellenmilieu als Verbrechensquelle." *Kriminalistik* 4: 147–153.

Part III
Queer intelligibility and unintelligibility

9 "No one talked about it"
The paradoxes of lesbian identity in pre-1989 Poland

Magdalena Staroszczyk

> This life wasn't my life at all. However . . . it was fine in an external sense. So calm and well-ordered: a husband, nice children, everything, everything. But it was external, and my life was not my life at all, it wasn't me.

These are the words of a 67-year-old Polish woman interviewed for the CRUSEV project, a study of queer cultures in the 1970s. What does it mean to live a life that is "not one's own"? What does it mean to reminisce about such a life decades later? And what does it mean to examine these memories in a cultural context that is dramatically different from the one remembered? This chapter tackles the question of lesbian existence and lesbian identity in the final decades of the People's Republic of Poland and briefly comments on the post-1989 political transition. I examine the experience and self-identification of non-heteronormative women, some who do not identify as lesbians and some who identify as lesbians today but in their narratives recall a time when they did not.

The question of lesbian visibility is pertinent today because of the limited number of lesbian-oriented activist events and cultural representations. But it presents a major methodological problem when looking at the past. That problem lies in an almost complete lack of historical sources, something partly mended with oral history interviews, but also in an epistemological dilemma. How can we talk about lesbians when they did not exist as a recognizable category? What did their (supposed) non-existence mean? And should we even call those who (supposedly) did not exist "lesbians"?

To illustrate this problem, let me begin with excerpts from an interview I conducted for the CRUSEV project. My interlocutor is a lesbian woman born in the 1950s, who lived in Cracow most of her life:

> To this very day I have a problem with my brothers, as I cannot talk to them about this. They just won't do it, I would like to talk, but. . . .

They have this problem, they lace up their mouths when any reference is made to this topic, because they were raised in that reality [when] no one talked about it. It was a taboo. It still is. . . .
I was so weak, unable to take initiative, lacking a concept of my own life—all this testifies to the oppression of homosexual persons, who do not know how to live, have no support from [others], no information or knowledge learned at school, or from a psychologist. What did I do? I searched in encyclopaedias for the single entry, "homosexuality." What did I learn? That I was a pervert. What did it do to me? It only hurt me, no?

Q: Was the word lesbian in use?
Only as a slur. Even my mother used it as an offensive word. When she finally figured out my orientation, she said the word a few times. With hatred. Hissing the word at me.

The woman offers shocking testimony of intense and persistent hostility towards a family member—sister, daughter—who happens to be a lesbian. The brothers and the mother are so profoundly unable to accept her sexuality that they cannot speak about it at all, least of all rationally. The taboo has remained firmly in place for decades. How was it maintained? And, perhaps more importantly, how do we access the emotional reality that it caused? The quotes all highlight the theme of language, silence, and something unspeakable. Tabooization implies a gap in representation, and the appropriate word cannot be spoken but merely hissed out with hatred.

Popular discourse and academic literature alike address this problem under the rubric of "lesbian invisibility" (Mizielińska 2001). I put forward a different conceptual frame, proposing to address the question of lesbian identity in pre-1989 Poland not in terms of visibility versus invisibility, but instead in terms of cultural intelligibility versus unintelligibility. The former concepts, which have a rich history in discussions of pre-emancipatory lesbian experience, presume an already existing identity that is self-evident to the person in question. They assume the existence of a person who thinks of herself as a lesbian. One then proceeds to ask whether or not this lesbian was visible as such to others, that is, whether others viewed her as the lesbian she knew she was. Another assumption behind this framing is that the woman in question wished to be visible although this desired visibility had been denied her. These are some of the essentializing assumptions inscribed in the concept of (in)visibility. Their limitation is that they only allow us to ask whether or not the lesbian is *seen* for who she feels she is and wishes to be seen by others.

By contrast, (un)intelligibility looks first to the social construction of identity, especially to the constitutive role of language. To think in those terms is to ask under what conditions same-sex desire between women is culturally legible as constitutive of an identity. So, instead of asking if people saw lesbians for who they really were, we will try to understand the specific epistemic conditions which made some women socially recognizable to others, and also to themselves, as "lesbians." This use of the concept "intelligibility" is analogous to its use by Judith Butler in *Gender Trouble*, as she explains why gender conformity is key to successful personhood:

> [T]he question here will be: To what extent do regulatory practices of gender formation and division constitute identity, the internal coherence of the subject, indeed, the self-identical status of the person? To what extent is "identity" a normative ideal rather than a descriptive feature of experience? And how do the regulatory practices that govern gender also govern culturally intelligible notions of identity? In other words, the "coherence" and "continuity" of "the person" are not logical or analytical features of personhood, but, rather, socially instituted and maintained norms of intelligibility. Inasmuch as "identity" is assured through the stabilizing concepts of sex, gender, and sexuality, the very notion of "the person" is called into question by the cultural emergence of those "incoherent" or "discontinuous" gendered beings who appear to be persons but who fail to conform to the gendered norms of cultural intelligibility by which persons are defined.
>
> (Butler 2002, 23)

For Butler, cultural intelligibility is thus an aspect of the social norm, as it corresponds to "a normative ideal." It is one of the conditions of coherence and continuity requisite for successful personhood. In a similar vein, to say that lesbians in the People's Republic of Poland were not culturally intelligible is of course not to claim that there were no women engaged in same-sex romantic and erotic relationships—such a conclusion would be absurd, as well as untrue. It is, rather, to suggest that "lesbian" was not a category of personhood available or, for that matter, desirable to many non-heteronormative women. The word was not in common use and it did not signify to them the sort of person they felt they were. Nor was another word readily available, as interlocutors' frequent periphrases strongly suggest, for example, "I cannot talk to them about *this*. . . . They . . . lace up their mouths when any reference is made to *this topic*" (my emphases).

Interviews conducted with women for the CRUSEV project are filled with pain due to rejection. So are the interviews conducted by Anna Laszuk, whose *Dziewczyny, wyjdźcie z szafy* (*Come Out of the Closet, Girls!* 2006) was a pioneering collection of herstories which gave voice to non-heteronormative Polish women of different ages, including those who remember the pre-1989 era. Lesbian unintelligibility is arguably a major theme in the collection. The pain caused by the sense of not belonging expressed by many illustrates that being unintelligible can be harmful. At the same time, unintelligibility had some practical advantages. The main among them was relative safety in a profoundly heteronormative society. As long as things went unnamed, a women-loving woman was not in danger of stigmatization or social ostracism.

Basia, born in 1939 and thus the oldest among Laszuk's interviewees, offers a reassuring narrative in which unintelligibility has a positive valence:

> I cannot say a bad word about my parents. They knew but they did not comment. . . . My parents never asked me personal questions, never exerted any kind of pressure on me to get married. They were people of great culture, very understanding, and they quite simply loved me. They would meet my various girlfriends, but these were never referred to as anything but "friends" (*przyjaciółki*). Girls had it much easier than boys because intimacy between girls was generally accepted. Nobody was surprised that I showed up with a woman, invited her home, held her hand, or that we went on trips together.
>
> (Laszuk 2006, 27)

The gap between visceral knowing and the impossibility of naming is especially striking in this passage. The parents "knew" and Basia knew that they knew, but they did not comment, ask questions, or make demands, and Basia clearly appreciates their silence as a favour. To her, it was a form of politeness, discreetness, perhaps even protectiveness. The silence was, in fact, a form of affectionate communication: "they quite simply loved me."

Another of Laszuk's interviewees is Nina, born around 1945 and 60 years old at the time of the interview. With a certain nostalgia, Nina recalls the days when certain things were left unnamed, suggesting that there is erotic potential in the unintelligibility of women's desire. Laszuk summarizes her views:

> Nina claims that those times certainly carried a certain charm: erotic relationships between women, veiled with understatement and secrecy, had a lot of beauty to them. Clandestine looks were exchanged above the heads of people who remained unaware of their meaning, as women understood each other with half a gesture, between words. Nowadays, everything has a name, everything is direct.
>
> (Laszuk 2006, 33)

A similar equation between secrecy and eroticism is drawn by the much younger Izabela Filipiak, trailblazing author of Polish feminist fiction in the 1990s and the very first woman in Poland to publicly come out as lesbian, in an interview for the Polish edition of *Cosmopolitan* in 1998. Six years later, Filipiak suggested a link between things remaining unnamed and erotic pleasure, and admitted to a certain nostalgia for this pre-emancipatory formula of lesbian (non)identity. Her avowed motivation was not the fear of stigmatization but a desire for erotic intensity:

> When love becomes passion in which I lose myself, I stop calculating, stop comparing, no longer anchor it in social relations, or some norm. I simply immerse myself in passion. My feelings condition and justify everything that happens from that point on. I do not reflect upon myself nor dwell on stigma because my feeling is so pure that it burns through and clears away everything that might attach to me as a woman who loves women.
>
> (Kulpa and Warkocki 2004)

Filipiak acknowledges the contemporary, "postmodern" (her word) lesbian identity which requires activism and entails enumerating various kinds of discrimination. But paradoxically—considering that she is the first public lesbian in Poland—she speaks with much more enthusiasm about the "modernist lesbians" described by Baudelaire:

> They chose the path of passion. Secrecy and passion. Of course, their passion becomes a form of consent to remain secret, to stay invisible to others, but this is not unambivalent. I once talked to such an "old-timer" who lived her entire life in just that way and she protested very strongly when I made a remark about hiding. Because, she says, she did not hide anything, she drove all around the city with her beloved and, of course, everyone knew. Yes, everyone knew, but nobody remembers it now, there is no trace of all that.
>
> (Kulpa and Warkocki 2004)

Cultural unintelligibility causes the gap between "everyone knew" and "nobody remembers" but it is also the source of excitement and pleasure. For Filipiak's "old-timer" and her predecessors, Baudelaire's modernist lesbians, the evasion, or rejection, of identity and the maintaining of secrecy is the path of passion. Crucially, these disavowals of identity mobilize a discourse of freedom rather than hiding, entrapment, or staying in the closet. The lack of a name is interpreted as an unmooring from language and a liberation from its norms.

Needless to say, cultural unintelligibility may also lead to profound torment and self-hatred. In the concept of nationhood generated by nationalists and by the Catholic Church in Poland, lesbians (seen stereotypically) are double outsiders whose exclusion from language is vital.[1] A repentant homosexual woman named Katarzyna offers her testimony in a Catholic self-help manual addressing those who wish to be cured of homosexuality. (It is irrelevant for my purpose whether the testimony is authentic; my interest is in the discursive construction of lesbian identity as literally impossible and nonexistent.) Katarzyna speaks about her search for love, her profound sense of guilt and her disgust with herself. The word "lesbian" is never used; her homosexuality is framed as confusion and as straying from her true desire for God. The origin of the pain is the woman's unintelligibility to herself:

> Only I knew how much despair there was in my life on account of being different. First, there was the sense of being torn apart when I realized how different my desires were from the appearance of my body. Despite the storm of homosexual desire, I was still a woman. Then, the question: What to do with myself? How to live?
>
> (Huk 1996, 121)

A woman cannot love other women—the subject knows this. We can speculate that her knowledge is due to her Catholic upbringing; she has internalized the teaching that homosexuality is a sin, and thus untrue and not real. The logic of the confession is overdetermined: the only way for her to become intelligible to herself is to abandon same-sex desire and turn to God, and through him to men. Church language thus frames homosexuality as chaos: it is a disordered space where no appropriate language can obtain. Within this frame, unintelligibility is anything but erotic. It is rather an instrument of shaming and, once internalized, a symptom of shame.

For many, the experience of unintelligibility is moored in intense heteronormativity, without regard to Church teachings or the language of national belonging. Struggling with the choice between social intelligibility available to straights and leading an authentic life outside the realm of intelligibility, one CRUSEV interlocutor, aged 67, describes her youth in 1960s and 1970s:

> I always knew I was a lesbian . . . and if I am one, then I will be one. Yes, in that sense. And not to live the life of a married woman, mother and so on. This life wasn't my life at all. However, as I said, it was fine in an external sense. So calm and well-ordered: a husband, nice

children, everything, everything. But it was external, and my life was not my life at all, it wasn't me.

She thus underscores her internal sense of dissonance, a felt incompatibility with the social role she was playing. The role model of a wife and mother was available to her, but a lesbian role model was not.

The discomfort felt at the unavailability of a role model may have had different consequences. Another CRUSEV interviewee, aged 62, describes her impulse to change her life so as to authentically experience her feelings for another woman, in contrast to that woman's ex:

> She visited me a few times, and it was enough that I wrote something, anything . . . [and] she would get on the train and travel across the country. There were no telephones then, during martial law. Regardless of anything, she would be there. And at one point I realized that I . . . damn, I loved her. . . . She broke up with her previous girlfriend very violently—this may interest you—because it turned out that the girl was so terribly afraid of being exposed and of some unimaginable consequences that she simply ran away.

The fear of exposure, critically addressed by the interlocutor, was nonetheless something she, too, experienced. She goes on to speak of "hiding a secret" and "stifling" her emotions.

A concern with leading an inauthentic life resurfaces in the account of the afore-quoted woman, aged 67:

> I couldn't reveal my secret to anyone. The only person who knew was my friend in Cracow. I led such a double life, I mean. . . . It is difficult to say if this was a life, because it was as if I had my inner spirituality and my inner world, entirely secret, but outside I behaved like all the other girls, so I went out with some boys. . . . It was always deeply suppressed by me and I was always fighting with myself. I mean, I fell in love [with women] and did everything to fall out of love [*laughter*]. On and on again.

Her anxiety translates into self-pathologizing behaviour:

> In 1971 I received my high school diploma and I was already . . . in a relationship of some years with my high school girlfriend. . . . But because we both thought we were abnormal, perverted or something, somehow we wanted to be cured, and so she was going to college to Cracow, and I to Poznań. We engaged in geographic therapy, so to speak.

The desire to "be cured" from homosexuality recurs in a number of interviews. Sometimes it has a factual dimension, as interlocutors describe having undergone psychotherapy and even reparative therapy—of course, to no avail.

Others decide to have a relationship with a woman after years spent in relationships with men. Referring to her female partner of 25 years, who had previously been married to a man, one of my interlocutors suggests that her partner had been disavowing her homosexual desires for many years before the two women's relationship began: "the truth is that H. had struggled with it for more than 20 years and she was probably not sure what was going on." Despite this presumed initial confusion, the women's relationship had already lasted for more than 25 years at the time I conducted the interview.

Recognizing one's homosexual desires did not necessarily have to be difficult or shocking. It was not for this woman, aged 66 at the time of the interview:

> It was obvious to me. I didn't, no, no, I didn't suppress it, I knew that [I was going], "Oh, such a nice girl, I like this one, with this one I want to be close, with that one I want to talk longer, with that one I want to spend time, with that one I want, for example, to embrace her neck or grab her hand".

Rather, what came as a shock was the unavailability of any social role or language corresponding to this felt desire that came as a shock. The woman continues:

> It turned out that I couldn't talk to anyone about it, that I couldn't tell anyone. I realized this when I grew up and watched my surroundings, family, friends, society. I saw that this topic was not there! If it's not there, how can I get it out of myself? I wasn't so brave.

The tabooization of homosexuality—its unintelligibility—is a recurring thread in these accounts; what varies is the extent to which it marred the subjects' self-perception.

The consequences of lesbian unintelligibility are felt long after the political transition, even in progressive communities such as the emerging Warsaw feminist movement of the mid-1990s, as in this account by a woman of 70, who had previously lived abroad:

> There was one person who was known to be a lesbian but she never showed up with a partner and one didn't know anything about her private life. Maybe if we had been closer. So, it all seemed different to

me from the way it was in the feminist circles in England [where] in conversations, in discussions this topic came up explicitly. I would say that there was a particular type of homophobia, the "this does not particularly concern us" of the majority. And then, after some time, some women began to address it but [still] there was no discussion about how different relationships may be, [no discussion] about diversity, or liquidity. There seemed to be a difference in consciousness. It was quite obvious to me that H. and I were together, but it wasn't obvious to other people.

For many non-heteronormative women, the post-1989 organizing, be it gay-lesbian or feminist, was the first environment in which they could begin to build a network of social relations based on their same-sex desire. Of course, in the People's Republic of Poland there were no official associations enabling such meetings, but neither were there informal groups for women. This marks a significant difference from men. Informal institutions for homosexual men did exist, often in the same locations as before the Second World War. Baths, cruising grounds, cafes, and private parties at people's homes allowed men to build social bonds. Unlike the men we interviewed, the women do not mention any places that let them construct such bonds. Feeling isolated appears to have been a fairly universal experience, as expressed by this woman, aged 67:

> I didn't know any lesbian or even a gay man or anyone at all. They were there around me but it was all so deeply hidden, I myself was so deeply hidden with my orientation, I was very careful that nobody would guess. I was very lonely.

The fact that in the 1990s it became possible to freely associate, establish organizations, and publish without censorship was a game-changer. Following some pre-1989 attempts at samizdat publications addressed to gay men and, to a lesser extent, lesbians, the 1990s saw a proliferation of such publications. The question of lesbian (un)intelligibility began to be addressed. A 1991 issue of the magazine *Inaczej* asks at the head of the first of three columns devoted to lesbians: "Are there any lesbians in Poland?" What follows is an open call from the first lesbian group in Cracow to other lesbian girls and women to come out and join the community. In the second column we find a depressing letter written by high school girls from Zielona Góra describing the unpleasant repercussions they met with after being "caught in the act" by their families. The letter ends with a warning: "'DIFFERENT' couples should be very careful, because the so called 'NORMAL PEOPLE' are capable of terrible things" (*Inaczej*, 7–8/1991).

The third column contains an even more dramatic letter by a woman from Russia (i.e. the Soviet Union in the process of dissolution) in which she describes being forcefully locked up in a psychiatric hospital as a lesbian and being medicated against her will with sedatives as part of conversion therapy. All three texts thus criticize lesbian unintelligibility as underlying actual violence against lesbian women and initiate the transition to intelligibility and visibility.

Ten years on, the socio-cultural landscape in Poland was changing rapidly due to activism. In 2003, the Campaign Against Homophobia held the nationwide campaign *Let Them See Us*, which presented 15 photos of lesbian and gay-male couples holding hands taken by the artist Katarzyna Breguła. The photos were exhibited in art galleries and mounted on billboards in four Polish cities. Anna Gruszczyńska, one of the organizers, says that the action was: "the most important moment, thanks to which there were more and more girls [visible in the public sphere]" (2005, 146). In 2004, the Lesbian Coalition was established as the first activist initiative dedicated exclusively to non-heterosexual women. Alicja Kowalska asserts that, unlike some earlier groups, which were smaller and less public, the Coalition was set up to fight for lesbian rights openly and to make lesbianism more visible. For example, in 2005 members of the Lesbian Coalition co-organized Manifa, the annual feminist march in Warsaw (Kowalska 2011). The years 2003–2005 thus mark the end of lesbian unintelligibility, as the question of their (in)visibility takes precedence.

Note

1 Joanna Mizielińska sums up the logic of lesbian exclusion: "They are women, but they are not mothers and are useless to the nation. Moreover, because they resist the traditional and 'natural' position of women, they threaten the 'universal' patriarchal order emphasized in national discourse. . . . Therefore, for the sake of the nation, lesbian existence must be either kept quiet or presented as deviant" (Mizielińska 2001, 283). Keeping lesbians quiet, that is, devoid of access to language, and presenting them as deviant, and thus undesirable also to themselves, are two ways of perpetuating their unintelligibility as persons belonging to the imagined community of the nation.

Bibliography

Butler, Judith. 2002. *Gender Trouble*. New York and London: Routledge.
"Czy w Polsce są lesbijki?" 1991. *Inaczej*: 7–8.
Gruszczyńska, Anna. 2005. "Komu można powiedzieć?" In *Feministki własnym głosem o sobie*, edited by Sławomira Walczewska. Kraków: Wydawnictwo Efka.
Huk, Tadeusz. 1996. *Kościół wobec homoseksualizmu*. Warszawa: Wydawnictwo Sióstr Loretanek.

Kowalska, Alicja. 2011. "Polish Queer Lesbianism: Sexual Identity Without a Lesbian Community." *Journal of Lesbian Studies* 15 (3): 324–336.
Kulpa, Robert, and Błażej Warkocki. 2004. "Poszukiwanie lustra. Rozmowa z Izabelą Filipiak o lesbijkach i literaturze lesbijskiej." *Kobiety kobietom*. Accessed 25 August 2019. https://kobiety-kobietom.com/queer/art.php?art=738.
Laszuk, Anna. 2006. *Dziewczyny, wyjdźcie z szafy!* Płock: Fundacja Lorga.
Mizielińska, Joanna. 2001. "The Rest Is Silence. Polish Nationalism and the Question of Lesbian Existence." *The European Journal of Women's Studies* 8 (3): 281–297.
Szcześniak, Magda. 2016. *Normy widzialności. Tożsamość w czasach transformacji*. Warszawa: Fundacja Bęc Zmiana.
Szulc, Łukasz. 2018. *Transnational Homosexuals in Communist Poland: Cross-Border Flows in Gay and Lesbian Magazines*. Cham: Palgrave Macmillan.
Tomasik, Krzysztof. 2006. *Homobiografie: pisarki i pisarze polscy XIX i XX wieku*. Warszawa: Wydawnictwo Krytyki Politycznej.
Tomasik, Krzysztof. 2018. *Gejerel. Mniejszości seksualne w PRL-u*. Warszawa: Wydawnictwo Krytyki Politycznej.

10 Queer (in)visibility in the art of the People's Republic of Poland

Karol Radziszewski and Wojciech Szymański

Introduction

The intent behind this chapter is to present a range of creative strategies and life choices among non-heteronormative artists in mid- to late People's Republic of Poland and to showcase some ways the artists were being discussed, frequently with homophobic clichés. Some of their work was originally perceived as amateurish rather than professional but was subsequently re-assessed. We intentionally avoid applying the "gay" label to our protagonists, Krzysztof Niemczyk, Krzysztof Jung, and Ryszard Kisiel, and neither do we refer to their output as "gay art." Despite how entrenched this naming has become, in the past decade or so, among Polish scholars of non-heteronormative legacy, it is patently anachronistic and thus ultimately flawed. It fails to reflect the pre-1980s context, a time before the English word "gay" (spelled *gej*) came into use, becoming an accepted identity label only during the 1990s. Kisiel, the only living artist of the three, is also the only one to ever describe himself as gay. This is not to say that we are pushing Niemczyk and Jung back into the closet. While not literally "gay," they were homosexual men and their psychosexual identity, we contend, was essential to their oeuvre. Their proto-gay, pre-liberation activities may be described as "non-heteronormative" and perhaps as "queer."

Our examples obviously do not exhaust the spectrum of the era. We picked three artists whom we find especially interesting, different from one another, yet mutually competitive, as well as relatable to developments in world art more broadly. Such analogies neither suggest the Polish artists' universality nor deny their originality. Insofar as there is a universalizing feature in our argument, it is the prevalence of homophobia in both the global East and the global West, their different economic and political systems notwithstanding.

In what follows, we discuss, first, the most radical, queer, anarchist, almost situationist performances/happenings by the iconoclastic Krzysztof Niemczyk. We then compare them with Krzysztof Jung's practices. Finally,

Queer (in)visibility 117

we present the progressive, subversive quotidian performances by Ryszard Kisiel—an amateur artist whose approach in some ways outdid the creative strategies of the other two.

Krzysztof Niemczyk: homosexual desire before gay liberation

Krzysztof Niemczyk (1938–1994) was an *artiste maudit*, a non-professional artist who never attended an art school, a living legend both celebrated and reviled, a regular patron of mental institutions and police detention centres. Such is the ballpark image in the testimony of those who knew him, reiterated in the early studies dating from the late twentieth/early twenty-first century, after this already-forgotten artist's death (see Wisłocki 2007, 279–286; Jackowska and Sipowicz 2007, 253–254; Ptaszkowska 2007, 259–272). Indeed, Niemczyk's turbulent life was marked with arrests and stays in mental institutions, and he never received regular academic training. This Warsaw-born artist lived and worked in Cracow throughout his life, where he enjoyed access to the close-knit community around Tadeusz Kantor, an artist wielding great symbolic authority at the time. Ultimately, it is Niemczyk's non-normative sexuality that has become central from the vantage point of gay and queer studies. His sexuality was addressed in his posthumous *Traktat o życiu Krzysztofa Niemczyka na użytek młodych pokoleń* (*Treaty on the Life of Krzysztof Niemczyk for the Edification of the Young*, 2007), the first major publication on the artist and one whose importance has not been surpassed. While Niemczyk's sexuality was not closeted, its precise status is ambiguous and has regularly been questioned. The volume encompasses Niemczyk's own writings, including never-before published personal documents (his letters and journals), accounts by friends and acquaintances, analyses of his literary and artistic pieces, and interviews. The artist's homosexuality and its influence on his work is only mentioned twice: in his journal and in an interview with his sister Monika Niemczyk, which she granted to the book's editors Piotr Marecki and Marcin Hernas, both of them junior scholars at the time.[1]

In all other instances, sexual intimacy between men is addressed metaphorically and it dissolves in the figure of the accursed artist: an eccentric hovering on the edges of regular life. Also in those passages in which Niemczyk's homosexuality is openly expressed, it appears as problematic and even shameful. When questioned by Marecki and Hernas, who say, "We have heard *reports* concerning his sexuality; some claim he was homosexual, others that he was bisexual," the artist's sister confirms, "Krzysztof was a homosexual," and adds, "Krzysztof wasn't secretive about it, *regrettably burdening us*, our mother and me, with very intimate details. He talked of his love for [Jacek] Gulla, of the suffering he was going through. Willy-nilly *we were forced to listen*" (2007, 224; our emphases). Anka Ptaszkowska's comment similarly implies that homosexuality was regarded as an intemperate and crime-like activity, linked somehow to paedophilia. Ptaszkowska, an art critic and Niemczyk's close friend, recalls the following encounter with the artist and a teenage minor whom he was helping out: "I remember Krzysztof and Jaś coming to see me in Zalesie to assure me that they were not having sex. Indeed, Jaś would later have a girlfriend in Paris" (Ptaszkowska 2007, 228).

The homophobic discourse engaged by Marecki and Hernas' interlocutors was reiterated in the book's critical reception, which was generally positive. For example, in a lecture delivered in 2009 and published in 2010, Ptaszkowska declared,

> Łukasz Maciejowski [Polish journalist and film critic] . . . accepted Niemczyk into the gay family as the one "who fought and died for us." The statement merits some clarification: while Niemczyk was openly homosexual, he was not gay, meaning he was not a member of a group founded on a sense of solidarity or a sense of belonging to a class of persons. Had someone told him he was expected to die for such a group, he would die laughing.
>
> (Ptaszkowska 2009, 168–169)

Ptaszkowska is right, in a sense: Niemczyk was not gay, not because he was heterosexual but because the word "gay" as a label of self-identity would only come into use much later, in the 1980s, to become the community's standard term at the turn of the 1980s and 1990s. Niemczyk was thus a homosexual, as this was the designation, however medicalizing or psychological, which he had at his disposal. Then again, the choice to even use this label was his to make. Ptaszkowska is thus correct and yet wrong when she engages in openly homophobic divagations about homosexuals as a distinct class, in unfortunate semblance to the present-day witch-hunt against "LGBT ideology," whose movers and shakers are quick to say that while they have nothing against homosexual individuals, they are battling against the gay movement and its rights-based discourse.

We may never know for a fact if Niemczyk would have begun identifying as gay had he lived longer and remained an active artist into the 1990s. In contrast to Ptaszkowska, however, we think that he might. Excerpts from his 1968 journals, preserved and now published, contain his ponderings on sexual liberation which fully coincide with the subsequent gay movement, describing the experience of any non-heteronormative person who ever suffered oppression or was forced to deny the integrity of his or her humanity.

Queer (in)visibility 119

While we are very much familiar with such experience, it remains alien to Ptaszkowska and some other heterosexual critics. The journal entry reads, "I love Jacek so much and in so many ways that I would be ready to relinquish him carnally if given the option to instead love him *openly*, with the full approval of friends and family, and with his tacit consent" (Niemczyk 2007, 28; our emphasis).

Our speculative hypothesis is also confirmed by Niemczyk's performative artworks in the second half of the 1960s. Interpreted through the prism of Situationism, with which these works were both co-synchronous and ideologically overlapping (Hernas and Marecki 2007, 273–278), and seen also from a point in time more than 50 years later, they merit recognition as pioneering queer performances in postwar Polish art. Indeed, their novelty made them so opaque that they have not been counted as artistic activity until the early days of our century. In 2010, Paweł Leszkowicz, who in turn pioneered Polish gay-focused research in art history, brilliantly interpreted Niemczyk's actions as intentionally performative artworks and identified their sexually revolutionary meanings (see Leszkowicz 2010, 20–23, 2012, 302–306). In particular, Leszkowicz read an action—or "situation," as named by editors of the *Traktat*—staged by the artist in Cracow in the second half of the 1960s (exact date is unknown) in the context of gay liberation. Niemczyk bathed, as it were, in a fountain located in Cracow's main square, the topographic and actual heart of the city. One Sunday morning, undressed, he entered the fountain pool, removed his underwear and presented his bare buttocks to an opportune audience: partly amused, one assumes, partly outraged, as they were filing out of St. Mary's Church after Sunday Mass.

Niemczyk's performance may indeed be interpreted as liberation from bourgeois conventions, from the invisibility of non-heteronormative persons in the Polish society and in the official culture of the time, as defined by state and Church, and from male nudity conventionalized by the artists themselves and deprived of all sexual aspect in favour of "academic" treatment of the body.[2] Yet, Niemczyk's action was also a situationist intervention *par excellence*, very much in Guy Debord's spirit of *détournement* and Raoul Vaneigem's revolution of everyday life. The act of anarchist disobedience (exhibitionism, bathing in public) breached the socialist (rather than capitalist) spectacle.

Yet liberation did not arrive at once, just as random onlookers did not see in Niemczyk's exhibitionist act the rebellion of a homosexual body or an artist's intervention in public space. They likely thought it a loutish stunt or the act of a mentally unstable person. Actions or happenings similar to Niemczyk's performance had only just seen the light of day. The medium was a novelty in Poland and elsewhere. Moreover, such events were typically organized within the confines of institutional art. For example, the well-known happenings by Tadeusz Kantor, an artist to whose circle Niemczyk belonged at the time, including the *Panoramic Sea Happening* (1967) and the earlier *Cricotage* (1965, considered the first of its kind in Poland), were organized in the presence of well-prepared viewers at locations determined by the institutional art world.[3]

Niemczyk's body—nude, precarious, helpless in the face of the authoritarian People's Republic of Poland and of the totally heterosexist cultural universe—was a queerly excessive, pre-liberation gesture protesting sexual oppression. In its way, it laid the ground for younger artists, including Krzysztof Jung, who debuted in the following decade.

Krzysztof Jung: art as space of liberty

Krzysztof Jung (1951–1998) was born in Warsaw, where he graduated from the Visual Graphics Faculty of the Academy of Fine Arts. He was a painter, graphic artist and performer associated with Warsaw's countercultural Repassage gallery, which he managed in 1978–1979 (see Sitkowska 2001). In the second half of the 1970s, he focused on performance art, especially on a series of activities involving the use of thread. He "threaded" together his own nude body and individual participants, the audience at large, objects, and the gallery space in various configurations. His actions addressed a small and trusted circle, and some were dedicated to particular persons.[4] From our vantage point, *Joint Performance* (1980, later repeated in a slightly altered version and renamed *Conversation*) seems especially interesting (see Sitkowska 2001). Jung both literally and metaphorically bound his body to that of another man, Wojciech Piotrowski (the artist's friend and partner at the time) in a manner akin to dialogue. Dressed in black trousers and black shirts, seated in chairs facing each other, the two men proceeded to sew their clothes together, to finally liberate themselves of all attire and leave the performance space in the nude. Their private relationship was not announced. The action was a metaphorical ritual: an abstract visualization of a relationship and of homoerotic tension.

Jung was interested in sensuality. A physically attractive man himself, he displayed his body willingly, even narcissistically. Yet, he did not perceive the predominantly male nudity he used in his performances as a violation of moral taboos (Jung 1993, 111). Nudity was a road to truth, nature, freedom, and sovereignty, a perfect match for the countercultural hippie mood of the times. Nor did Jung ever comment on his own sexuality but kept it ambivalent, enjoying the freedom afforded by the open-minded community of Repassage and of his own circle of friends. These friends often visited his summer house, called "Jungówka" after his surname, which the artist Grzegorz Kowalski describes as a marvellously liberated space where everyone was in the nude and could be fully him- or herself.[5]

As noted by Leszkowicz (2017, 45), who consistently refers to Jung as "precursor of Polish gay art" (2010, 16), the homosexual eroticism "concealed" in his work was likely visible to those who were witnessing his actions.[6] Nonetheless, recorded comments and testimony contain merely hints and allusions. Remarks about the threadings, including by Jung himself, resort to all kinds of rhetorical manoeuvres and Aesopian language to avoid naming his non-normative sexuality. Leszkowicz points out that prudish speech prevails in the two exhibition catalogues.[7] Karol Sienkiewicz criticized such omissions in his review of the more recent exhibition "Krzysztof Jung. Przemiana" ("Krzysztof Jung. The Transformation," 2016), held at the Salon of the Academy of Fine Arts in Warsaw. He wrote, "Understandable decades ago, such silence is striking today" (Sienkiewicz 2016). Asked about this criticism, Grzegorz Kowalski, one of Jung's closest friends and a man instrumental to how Jung is remembered, argues that Jung always insisted his art was a "universal whole."[8] Kowalski accuses scholars who attempt to read Jung's work from a queering perspective of reductionistic fragmenting of his integral body of work and he disparagingly calls them "activists of the gay liberation movement," a phrase which presumably applies to Sienkiewicz and the authors of this chapter. Kowalski sees our disagreement as a generational difference:

> We accepted a closeted life, though perhaps it was not closeted, back in the 1980s. It gave us the sense that we were living fully. We were not lacking anything here. Or if we were, one travelled to Berlin or Paris, and Krzysztof would bring back whatever was missing; whereas you guys—as Karol Sienkiewicz explicitly said in his article on the Academy Salon—believe that Jung will only be recognised as an artistic icon if his work is openly classified as queer. Although it was not. I think Jung aspired to making his art universal. Such was his ambition—maybe he has to be so reduced today in order to reemerge as a queer artist.[9]

Another instance of Jung's ambivalent status, of this hovering between visibility and invisibility, are the gay porn tapes he collected during his travels across Western Europe.[10] It goes without saying that watching pornography is usually considered a fully private and non-artistic activity. Yet, as recalled by Adam Adach, painter and friend of the artist, Jung would organize pornographic film screenings for his friends (both homo- and heterosexual), events which Adach attended, and which frequently doubled as parties with refreshments served.[11] Participants of these porn-watching sessions would debate the cinematography, note the country of origin, the director, the actors, and the storyline.[12] Such screenings, absurd at first glance, may be interpreted as performative art events and intentionally campy happenings. Although camp, a key term for non-normative queer aesthetics, would not become an object of academic interest in Poland until the turn of the century, the influence of Susan Sontag's 1964 "Notes on Camp" seems clear in the screenings Jung organized.[13] Sontag's essay was first published in Polish in 1979 (by *Literatura na Świecie*, an influential monthly with a cult following, devoted to international literature). Notably, Sontag included "stag movies seen without lust" into the camp canon (1999, 55). Situations designed by Jung to provoke intellectual deliberation on pornography and, by extension, on the agonistic relationship between the visible and the concealed, are a great example of the camp mode of perceiving and experiencing the world.

Unexpectedly for us, a poignant epilogue to our deliberation on the tension between the "visible" and the "concealed" aspects of Jung's art came in 2019 in the form of an exhibition of the artist's work at the Schwules Museum in Berlin.[14] The show, initiated by Jung's ex-partner, the writer and art historian Wojciech Karpiński, was accompanied by a richly illustrated catalogue, somewhat tendentiously titled *The Male Nude*. The curator Wolfgang Theis' essay references the entire homosexual pantheon, including St. Sebastian, Constantine Cavafy, and David Hockney, placing Jung within the well-established frame of "high gay art," a trope available in the global East and the global West (see Sienkiewicz 2019). An analogous point is made by Raimund Wolfert, who wrote the second essay in the catalogue, titled "A Flame: Krzysztof Jung, a Precursor of Polish Gay Art."[15] While Jung's performances were subversively queer and understated, the exhibition referenced them only in passing in the form of small-size reproductions positioned near the entrance. The show focused primarily on Jung's homoerotic drawings, a series inspired by St. Sebastian's iconography. The drawings were found posthumously in the artist's desk and were shown in such a massive selection for the first time.[16] The exhibition thus neglected other aspects of Jung's oeuvre. Theis (2019, 20) notes that Karpiński first approached the museum as early as in 2001 but the show was delayed because of the institution's other plans and commitments.

To our knowledge, there are no plans to bring the exhibition to Poland. It would thus seem that Jung's personal interest in sexuality can only be openly addressed in the so-called West, whereas in his homeland the Aesopian language of metaphor and allusion persists for the sake of protecting his memory.[17] We must still wait for an in-depth reading of Jung which would overcome this polarity.

Ryszard Kisiel: life as a work of art and queer everyday performance

Ryszard Kisiel's activities afford an interesting context to Jung's oeuvre and its reception. Nearly Jung's coeval, Kisiel was born in Gdańsk in 1948, son of a seaman and a nun (Radziszewski and Kubara 2011, 28–39). He did not aspire to be an artist, seeing the photography he had pursued since the late 1960s as a hobby. From early on he was focusing on self-portraits, usually in the nude, and taking nudes of friends and acquaintances, and of patrons of nude beaches in Poland and Bulgaria.

Ever since the 1970s, Kisiel has been active in the homosexual community in Gdańsk, which we might describe as "queer before gay," to quote Douglas Crimp (see Danbolt 2008). Kisiel recalls in conversation that upon hearing of the gay liberation movement in the 1970s, he and a friend wondered what it might mean in the context of the People's Republic of Poland.[18] Penalization of homosexual acts had been abolished back in 1932, and postwar Poland was the only Eastern Bloc country not to have or reintroduce the ban. No doubt the society was homophobic and the socialist authorities' puritanism, together with the immensely influential Catholic Church, was setting the moral tone, but homosexuals were not being imprisoned, unlike in neighbouring countries. In the mid-1980s, however, the nationwide and long-lasting Operation Hyacinth, staged by the state police with the intent to gather information on homosexuals and their community, became a watershed for Kisiel. Officially, the surveillance was meant to protect homosexuals in view of a growing rate of crime targeting non-heterosexual persons and in the face of the AIDS epidemic. In the years 1985–1987, Operation Hyacinth led to the creation of about 11,000 police records, each of them a file on an individual identified as homosexual (Majewska 2018; see also Morawska in this volume). The Operation triggered a panic response among the community, with witnesses recalling its repressive nature and attempts to coerce them into collaboration by blackmail. But the crackdown also prompted a liberatory impulse. To quote Kisiel, "since they began exposing our lifestyle, living in hiding made no sense anymore. Since we had nothing to lose, we decided to do our thing and worry about nothing" (Radziszewski 2009). In direct response to police persecution, Kisiel began publishing a zine titled *Filo*—one of the first queer periodicals in Central and Eastern Europe, semi-legally distributed among circles of friends from 1986 till 1989. After the 1989 transition, *Filo* became a regular magazine available at newsstands (Radziszewski and Kubara 2011; Szulc 2018). The group responsible for the samizdat publication and its readers may well be considered one of the first organized protogay communities in Poland (see Szcześniak 2016).

Apart from *Filo*, Kisiel and his friends engaged in a more relaxed form of subversive activity. They would gather in a flat owned by one of them and engage in photographic sessions, acting out queer fantasies and desires. Over several months in late 1985 and early 1986,[19] they created series of transparencies, rediscovered years later, which offer visual testimony to overcome some stereotypes about the era (see Basiuk 2011). Trouncing the image of homosexuals as hounded victims, they reveal considerable potential of positive energy, irony (also with regard to such taboo topics as AIDS), and—first and foremost—self-irony. The photo collection consists of several groups of pictures, among which the intentionally conceptual and pun-based mock "opening credits" is especially spectacular: in this long series of would-be cinematic stills, captions have been glued directly onto the nude body of an individual named Waldek, a blue-collar worker who was Kisiel's model and lover. Other series of photos include nude and dress-up sessions, such as *Badziewianka* (Trashie), *Indianka-Szamanka* (Indian-Shaman), and *Fakir*. There are also private shots of Kisiel's lover in a forest thicket, frames from a Bulgarian nude beach, and making-of photographs of the proper sessions.[20]

In the early 1980s, Kisiel began travelling across Poland and abroad, usually by train. He visited Poland's main cities: Warsaw, Cracow, Łódź, Katowice, Wrocław, and some provincial towns: Płock, Radom, Słupsk, and Kutno. He also journeyed to other Eastern Bloc countries: Czechoslovakia, Bulgaria, the German Democratic Republic, and Hungary. He travelled in real space but also among phantasms. Although he took multiple analogue photographs documenting the venues he visited, conventional tourist sights are not among them. When in Prague, he ignored the Hradcany Castle and Mala Strana, focusing instead on bars, public baths, parks, and all sorts of pickup spots and public meeting places used by homosexuals—the cruising sites of the 1970s and 1980s (see Burszta in this volume).

Many photographs are accompanied by informative captions. Kisiel intended the snapshots and the descriptions of the places for his never-completed grand project, to which he gave the English-language working title *Polish Gay Guide on the Europeans Socialists Countries* [sic]. The guidebook, which exists in manuscript, is a unique undertaking, valuable and hugely interesting. It is much more than an account of Kisiel's voyage across Central Europe's cruising sites. More to the point, it maps the life and culture of a community existing on the brinks of society in the 1970s and 1980s, tracing a way of life and a culture already in the past and yet neglected in sociological and historical research. Kisiel's photographs and descriptions fascinate because they are the only known integral record of the underground practices of non-heteronormative individuals to have survived from that place and time, undocumented anywhere else except, possibly, in state police archives.

The guidebook, including the word "gay" in its title, testifies both to an attempt at self-identification and to a more extensive, identity-related, political-emancipatory project. Kisiel seems to have been about a decade ahead of his times and a harbinger of what was to come. In the drab reality of state socialism, the broken English of his title and especially the word "gay" ushers in the new paradigm of identity politics, West-oriented and typical for the post-1989 period. With this usage, Kisiel fast-forwarded to the 1990s with its affirmative re-evaluation of sexual minorities. At the same time, he was not photographing pre-gay cruising sites as historical venues; on the contrary, he was documenting them as thriving underground institutions with the avowed intent to create a guidebook and a practical manual for others.

Kisiel's broad-scale project needs to also be recognized as an artwork. Kisiel was not a professional artist, nor has he subsequently become one. Nonetheless, his project may be interpreted today in the context of conceptual photography and as a visual-textual activity documenting and performing the reality it represents. Kisiel's expression of untethered sexuality (countering the ever-alive Polish sexophobia), his immense self-awareness, and sense of distance prompt us to think of his project as continuing Niemczyk's radical activities. While Kisiel had not been familiar with Niemczyk's work at the time, his strategies of resistance bring to mind Niemczyk's anarchist sexuality, in contrast to Jung's equivocation. Partly similar to Niemczyk's reception, Kisiel's openly queer images and performances, unprecedented in Polish culture at the time of their creation, have for many years remained invisible and unresearched, mainly because they were not considered part of professional artistic practice.[21] Only recently have they become a point of interest for Polish art historians and other scholars.[22]

Notes

1 Niemczyk writes openly about his same-sex erotic and sexual life in the published extracts from his journal of 1968 (see Niemczyk 2007, 28–29).
2 In that period the naked male body was present in the classical and traditional academic education—in studies of nature. However, in the 1970s it became recognized as the desexualized, socially and artistically engaged body of a performer—a medium rather than a subject. Niemczyk's performance is unique also in this context.
3 The *Panoramic Sea Happening* took place during an *en plein air* in Osieka, and *Cricotage* was presented in a Society of Friends of Fine Arts café in Chmielna street in Warsaw.
4 "Like the one described by Basia Turkiewicz-Gutt, which was absolutely dedicated to his ex, or would-be lover, who was sitting there and remained completely indifferent to the entire aura created by Krzysiek. And the others were merely witnesses"—remembers Grzegorz Kowalski, in an interview recorded by Karol Radziszewski on 22 August 2017.

5 Interview with Grzegorz Kowalski on 22 August 2017.
6 However, in a following paragraph, after having listed the characteristic features of "gay art," Leszkowicz writes that Jung "would be therefore a precursor of queer art in the Polish version," which is a completely unfounded and inexplicable equation of gay art with queer art. Leszkowicz had also presented Jung's work on the "Ars Homo Erotica" exhibition (see Leszkowicz 2010).
7 Leszkowicz refers to the catalogue of a retrospective exhibition dedicated to *Repassage*, which was presented in the Zachęta Gallery in 1993, and to the catalogue of Jung's monographic exhibition at the Xawery Dunikowski Museum of Sculpture in 2001 (Sitkowska 1993, 2001), as well as to recollections about Jung published after his death in *Zeszyty Literackie* ("Retrospektywa Krzysztof Jung (1951–1998)" 1999).
8 Interview with Grzegorz Kowalski on 22 August 2017.
9 Interview with Grzegorz Kowalski on 22 August 2017.
10 These travels—especially to Sweden, Berlin, and Paris—were an important element of both Jung's artistic education and the shaping of his homosexual identity.
11 Conversation with Karol Radziszewski during "A Night with Cassettes," an event that was part of the seventh edition of the queer festival "Pomada" on 30 September 2017.
12 This collection of several dozen cassettes are the only items that Grzegorz Kowalski had decided to keep after Jung's death. Kowalski donated them to the Queer Archives Institute.
13 We are not arguing that it was Jung's intention to create a camp experience of pornography as depicted by Sontag in "Notes on 'Camp'." Rather, we are pointing to the essentially transnational character of queer taste in the twentieth century.
14 Wolfgang Theis' exhibition titled *Krzysztof Jung 1951–1998. Drawings* was presented at the Schwules Museum in Berlin between 6 March–1 July 2019.
15 Wolfert—ostentatiously, as did Ptaszkowska in Niemczyk's case—mentions that Jung himself would have certainly objected to being included in the "gay art" frame.
16 In 1983, after being persuaded by Karpiński, and after becoming acquainted with Józef Czapski, Jung turned to traditional methods such as painting, drawing, and graphics. He was primarily interested in landscape painting, relying on strong, saturated colours and on symbolic meanings.
17 Although Karol Sienkiewicz, present at the exhibition opening, notes: "However, Jung is a bit infantilised here. The atmosphere—after all, of understatement, of pushing the gay out of the closet, but only slightly (because he did not want it, according to some undefined friends)—was unbearable" (Sienkiewicz 2016).
18 Ryszard Kisiel in conversation with Karol Radziszewski, 2017.
19 Kisiel states in the film *Kisieland* that the sessions were also a direct reaction to the Operation Hyacinth.
20 One of the co-creators of the stills was Henryk Sokalski (who also illustrated *Filo* under the pseudonym "Heinrich"), the only artist in the group who was educated in an art school. A decade after Radziszewski had revealed the photographs in his film and in numerous exhibitions, Sokalski finally agreed to sign them with his real name (previously, he had asked for anonymity, since he was afraid of losing his job in a highly homophobic workplace).

21 Whereas Jung used stills from this period while working on classical drawings or paintings, they are the definitive form for Kisiel. Furthermore, the camp masquerade and openly queer expression that characterizes Kisiel's stills is vastly different from Jung's modernist work.

22 Significantly, Leszkowicz fails to mention Kisiel in his pioneering scholarship, nor did he invite him to participate in the "Ars Homo Erotica" exhibition-manifesto, curated for the National Museum in Warsaw (2010).

Bibliography

Basiuk, Tomasz. 2011. "Notes on Radziszewski's *Kisieland*." In *The Archive as Project: The Poetics and Politics of the (Photo)archive*, edited by Krzysztof Pijarski, 470–481. Warszawa: Fundacja Archeologii Fotografii.

"Bo on sobie zrobił teatr . . . O życiu Krzysztofa Niemczyka opowiadają: siostra Monika szewczyk oraz przyjaciele—Anka Ptaszkowska i Tomek Wawak. Rozmawiają Piotr Marecki i Marcin Hernas." 2007. In *Traktat o życiu Krzysztofa Niemczyka na użytek przyszłych pokoleń*, edited by Anka Ptaszkowska, Marcin Harnas, and Piotr Marecki, 211–231. Kraków: Korporacja Ha!art.

Danbolt, Mathias. 2008. "Front Room—Back Room: An Interview with Douglas Crimp." *Trickster. Nordic Queer Journal* 2. http://trikster.net/2/crimp/1.html.

Hernas, Marcin, and Piotr Marecki. 2007. "Sytuacjonizm Niemczyka." In *Traktat o życiu Krzysztofa Niemczyka na użytek przyszłych pokoleń*, edited by Anka Ptaszkowska, Marcin Harnas, and Piotr Marecki, 273–278. Kraków: Korporacja Ha!art.

Interview with Grzegorz Kowalski on 22 August 2017, conducted and recorded by Karol Radziszewski.

Jackowska, Kora, and Kamil Sipowicz. 2007. "Bohater naszej młodości." In *Traktat o życiu Krzysztofa Niemczyka na użytek przyszłych pokoleń*, edited by Anka Ptaszkowska, Marcin Harnas, and Piotr Marecki, 253–254. Kraków: Korporacja Ha!art.

Jung, Krzysztof. 1993. "Repassage 2." In *Galeria Repassage, Repassage 2, ReRepassage, Sigma*, edited by Maryla Sitkowska, 109–117. Warszawa: Galeria Zachęta.

Leszkowicz, Paweł. 2010. *Art Pride: Gay Art from Poland*. Translated by Marcin Łakomski. Warszawa: Abiekt.pl.

Leszkowicz, Paweł. 2012. *Nagi mężczyzna. Akt męski w sztuce polskiej po 1945 roku*. Poznań: Wydawnictwo Naukowe UAM.

Leszkowicz, Paweł. 2017. "Balety w sieci niedopowiedzeń. Jung i sztuka gejowska." In *Krzysztof Jung. Przemiana*, edited by Jakub Zgierski, 43–69. Warszawa: Akademia Sztuk Pięknych w Warszawie.

Majewska, Ewa. 2018. "Public Against Our Will? The Caring Gaze of Leviathan, 'Pink Files' from the 1980s Poland and the Issue of Privacy." *InterAlia* 13: 54–77.

Niemczyk, Krzysztof. 2007. "Dziennik 1968." In *Traktat o życiu Krzysztofa Niemczyka na użytek przyszłych pokoleń*, edited by Anka Ptaszkowska, Marcin Harnas, and Piotr Marecki, 25–46. Kraków: Korporacja Ha!art.

Ptaszkowska, Anka. 2007. "Niemczyk i awangarda artystyczna." In *Traktat o życiu Krzysztofa Niemczyka na użytek przyszłych pokoleń*, edited by Anka Ptaszkowska, Marcin Harnas, and Piotr Marecki, 259–272. Kraków: Korporacja Ha!art.

Ptaszkowska, Anka. 2009. "Wykład o Niemczyku." In *Wierzę w wolność, ale nie nazywam się Beethoven*, 168–175. Gdańsk: słowo/obraz terytoria.

Radziszewski, Karol, dir. 2009. Kisieland. Art film.

"Retrospektywa Krzysztof Jung (1951–1998)." 1999. *Zeszyty Literackie* 67 (3): 111–124.

"Ryszard Kisiel. Interview by Karol Radziszewski and Paweł Kubara." 2011. *DIK Fagazine* 8: 28–39.

Sienkiewicz, Karol. 2016. "Artysta, faun, gej." *Dwutygodnik* 197. www.dwutygodnik.com/artykul/6822-artysta-faun-gej.html.

Sienkiewicz, Karol. 2019. *Jung w Schwules Museum*. https://sienkiewiczkarol.org/2019/03/27/jung-w-schwules-museum/.

Sitkowska, Maryla, ed. 1993. *Galeria Repassage, Repassage 2, ReRepassage, Sigma*. Warszawa: Galeria Zachęta.

Sitkowska, Maryla, ed. 2001. *Krzysztof Jung (1951–1998)*. Warszawa: Muzeum im. Xawerego Dunikowskiego w Królikarni—Oddział Muzeum Narodowego w Warszawie.

Sontag, Susan. 1999 (1964). "Notes on 'Camp'." In *Camp: Queer Aesthetics and the Performing Subject: A Reader*, edited by Fabio Cleto, 53–65. Ann Arbor: The University of Michigan Press.

Szcześniak, Magda. 2016. *Normy widzialności. Tożsamość w czasach transformacji*. Warszawa: Fundacja Bęc Zmiana.

Szulc, Łukasz. 2018 (2017). *Transnational Homosexuals in Communist Poland: Cross-Border Flows in Gay and Lesbian Magazines*. New York: Palgrave Macmillan.

Theis, Wolfgang. 2019. "Bedcovers, Pissoirs, Naked Saints and Self-Exploration." In *Krzysztof Jung: The Male Nude*, edited by Wojciech Karpiński and Mikołaj Nowak-Rogoziński, 15–22. Berlin: Schwules Museum.

Wisłocki, Seweryn A. 2007. "Fatalny autograf Allena Ginsberga." In *Traktat o życiu Krzysztofa Niemczyka na użytek przyszłych pokoleń*, edited by Anka Ptaszkowska, Marcin Harnas, and Piotr Marecki, 279–285. Kraków: Korporacja Ha!art.

Wolfert, Raimund. 2019. "A Flame. Krzysztof Jung, a Precursor of Polish Gay Art." Trans. Maya Latynski. In *Krzysztof Jung: The Male Nude*, edited by Wojciech Karpiński and Mikołaj Nowak-Rogoziński, 37–47. Berlin: Schwules Museum.

Index

Adler, Alfred 37
apartment civilization 17–20
archive 5, 11, 33, 41–42, 91
assimilation 45–48

Baldwin, James 23–27
ball 17–19, 21, 64, 11, 121
bathhouse 5, 15–16, 46
Berlin Wall 47
Berman, Paul 35
Biuletyn (quarterly, renamed *Etap*) 21, 24–25, 30
Butler, Judith 6, 107

camp 4, 51, 53, 122, 126
Campaign Against Homophobia 47, 114
Catholic Church 2, 75, 110, 123
Ciemiński, Ryszard 39
Cold War 62–63, 65
coming out 12, 20, 27–28, 116
Criminal Code of 1932 1, 34
criminology 91, 94, 99
Crimp, Douglas 4–5, 123
cruising grounds (and Polish *pikieta*) 1, 5, 11–16, 19–21, 46, 53, 94–97, 113, 124–125
CRUSEV (research project) 5, 41, 85, 105, 107, 110–111
cultural intelligibility *see* intelligibility

Darski, Krzysztof T. *see* Prorok, Dariusz
Delany, Samuel R. 16
drag queen 19, 48

Duggan, Lisa 48
Dulko, Stanisław 59–60, 67–69

Eastern European Information Pool 30, 64, 97
EEIP *see* Eastern European Information Pool
Etap (periodical) *see* Biuletyn

Fiedotow, Agata 2, 11, 90–91
Fik, Ignacy 37–38, 42
Filipiak, Izabela 109
Filo (periodical) 21, 123–124, 126

gay (and Polish *gej*) 4–5, 17–18, 21, 25, 41, 47–48, 53, 84–85, 116, 118, 125
gay parlours 5, 17–19, 21
gej see gay
Ghodsee, Kristen 62–63, 65
Giedroyc, Jerzy 36
Gombrowicz, Witold 34, 36–38, 41
Gorgol, Tadeusz 30
Gothic literature 5, 34, 36–38
Grabowska, Magdalena 34, 62, 65

Haan, Francesca de 62–63
Healey, Dan 1–2
hermaphrodite (archaic) 53, 61
Hernas, Marcin 117–118
heteronormativity 3, 13, 38, 48, 50–53, 70, 76, 78, 108, 110
"Hiacynt" *see* Operation Hyacinth
HIV/AIDS 2, 18, 24, 46, 50, 81, 123, 124

Index

Hocquenghem, Guy 40
homoeroticism 5, 24, 91, 120, 122
homonormativity 48–50, 53
homosexual closet 20, 27–29, 38, 99, 107, 116, 126
"homosexual phenomenon" 89, 91, 98
Homosexuals in the Church (organization) 64
Homosexuelle Initiative (HOSI Wien) 24, 30
Humphreys, Laud 13–14
Hyacinth see Operation Hyacinth

Imieliński, Kazimierz 59–60, 66–68, 70, 77, 94
Inaczej (periodical) 30, 31, 40, 41, 113
Institute for National Remembrance 88–91
intelligibility 6, 41, 83, 106–110, 112–114
Iron Curtain 3, 24, 30, 46, 62–63

Janion, Maria 6, 33–41
Jaworski, Marek see Selerowicz, Andrzej
Jung, Krzysztof 6, 116, 120–122, 126–127

Karpiński, Wojciech 122, 126
Kępiński, Tadeusz 38
Kisiel, Ryszard 6, 12, 116, 123–125, 126–127
Komornicka, Maria 33, 40
Kowalski, Grzegorz 121, 125, 126

Laszuk, Anna 107–108
lesbian (and Polish *lesbijka*) 4, 6, 21, 53, 81–84, 85, 91, 105–107, 109–111, 113–114
Lesbian Coalition 114
lesbijka see lesbian
Leszkowicz, Paweł 119, 121, 126–127
Lew-Starowicz, Zbigniew 6, 74, 76–85
Lovetown see *Lubiewo*
Lubiewo (novel) 6, 45–53
luj see thug

Magazyn Kochających Inaczej see *Inaczej*
Majewska, Ewa 2, 89, 91

Makarewicz's Code see Criminal Code of 1932
Marecki, Piotr 117–119
Martin, William 47, 50–52
Mayer, Hans 40
Milicja Obywatelska (*MO*) see police
Ministry of Internal Affairs 88–89, 91, 94, 99
Mizielińska, Joanna 4, 41, 46–47, 62, 65, 70, 106, 114
Money, John 66
Montherlant, Henry de 28–29
Muñoz, José Esteban 5

Nasalik, Madaleine 48, 50–52
Nedbálková, Kateřina 97
Niemczyk, Krzysztof 6, 116, 117–120, 125
Niewieski, Z. see Gombrowicz, Witold
Niziołek, Grzegorz 2

Odmieńcy (book) 33–34, 38–42
odmieniec see queer
Operation After Shave 97
Operation Brother 97
Operation Hyacinth ("Hiacynt") 2, 6, 30, 34, 81, 89–91, 95–99, 123, 126
oral history 5, 11, 23, 90, 93, 96–97, 105

Pankowski, Rudolf 24
patriarchy 53, 71, 114
People's Republic of Poland 1–3, 17, 24, 90, 113, 123
Pietkiewicz, Ewa 30
pikieta see cruising grounds
police 2, 6, 13, 30, 64, 88–99, 123
Polish United Workers' Party 39
Polish Supreme Court 61, 67–68
Polityka (weekly) 25, 30, 41
pornography 16, 18, 24, 39, 93–94, 121–122, 126
pre-emancipatory 6, 12, 45, 50, 106, 109
Prorok, Dariusz (aka. Krzysztof T. Darski) 25–27, 29–30, 41
prostitution 1, 34, 92, 94–95
proto-gay 3, 116, 123
proto-political 3, 30
Ptaszkowska, Anka 117–119, 126

queer (*odmieniec*) 1–6, 11–21, 23–25, 30, 33–34, 36–42, 45–54, 74, 76–77, 79, 81, 84, 90, 105, 116–117, 119–125; queer artefacts 18; queer translation 47–53
Queer Archives Institute 126

Relaks i Kolekcjoner Polski (periodical) 96
Repassage (art gallery) 120, 126
repression 38, 67, 69, 89–90, 123
respectability 14, 21
Revisionist Feminist Scholars 62
Rubin, Gayle 70, 77

Second World War 1, 16, 36, 66, 85, 113
Security Service of the Ministry of Internal Affairs 88, 90, 99
Sedgwick, Eve Kosofsky 23, 30, 34, 37–38
Selerowicz, Andrzej (aka. Marek Jaworski) 24–25, 27, 30, 89, 99
self-identification 20, 105, 125
self-organizing 5, 93, 95, 98
sex crime 92–93
sexual citizenship 13, 71
sexual inversion 91
Sienkiewicz, Karol 121–122, 126
Situationism 119
socialism 2, 11, 19, 61–62, 66, 75, 84, 125
Sontag, Susan 122, 126

Soviet Union (USSR) 1–2, 24, 28, 30, 63, 72, 75, 85, 97, 114
surveillance 2, 88–95, 123
Szulc, Łukasz 3, 11, 19, 21, 23, 24, 34, 41, 47, 62–64, 78, 81, 84, 89, 97, 123

taboo 39, 45, 90, 106, 112, 120, 124
theatre 2, 16, 18, 21, 28, 30
thug (and Polish *luj* or *żul*) 13, 98
Tomasik, Krzysztof xii, 3, 11, 17, 19, 89, 91, 94, 98–99
transgender 3–4, 33, 47, 48, 60–62, 66–71, 72; *see also* transsexualism
Transgresje (book series) 6, 33–34, 39–42
translation, literary 23–25, 29–30, 33, 40, 47–53
transsexualism (archaic) 59–62, 68, 70–71; *see also* transgender

UN Decade for Women 63

visibility 6, 20, 47, 89, 105–106, 114, 121

Warner, Michael 2
West/Western 6, 17–19, 24–25, 30, 34–35, 40, 46–47, 53, 61–67, 75, 78–79, 85, 116, 122, 125
Witkowski, Michał 6, 45–46, 52
W Służbie Narodu (periodical) 98

Zboralski, Waldemar 98
żul see thug

Printed in the United States
by Baker & Taylor Publisher Services